More Than a Meal

Abigail at United Poultry Concerns' Thanksgiving Party
Saturday, November 22, 1997
Photo: Barbara Davidson, The *Washington Times*, 11/27/97

More Than a Meal

*The Turkey in History, Myth,
Ritual, and Reality*

Karen Davis, Ph.D.

Lantern Books • New York
A Division of Booklight Inc.

Lantern Books
One Union Square West, Suite 201
New York, NY 10003

Printed in the United States of America

Library of Congress Cataloging-in-Publication Data

Davis, Karen, 1944–
  More than a meal : the turkey in history, myth, ritual, and reality / Karen Davis.
      p. cm.
Includes bibliographical references (p.   ).
  ISBN 1-930051-88-3 (alk. paper)
  1. Turkeys. I. Title.
  QL696.G27 D38 2001
  598.6'45—dc21

                                                          2001050343

For Boris, who "almost got to be
The real turkey inside of me."
From Boris, *by Terry Kleeman and Marie Gleason*

Credit: Susan Rayfield

Anne Shirley, 16-year-old star of "Anne of Green Gables" (RKO-Radio)
on Thanksgiving Day, 1934
Photo: Underwood & Underwood, © 1988 Underwood Photo Archives, Ltd., San Francisco

Table of Contents ~~

Acknowledgments ⁓

ONE OF THE MOST SATISFYING THINGS ABOUT my organization, United Poultry Concerns, is the wealth of material that people regularly send to my attention regarding birds and other matters of ultimate importance. I would like to thank everyone who thus indispensably contributed to the writing of this book as well as the invaluable people whom I specifically engaged to assist in the book's preparation.

They are: David Cantor, who tracked down and commented incisively on a variety of Thanksgiving articles and advertisements that appeared in the 20th century; Katy Otto, who made research for my book the focus of her Independent Study in journalism at the University of Maryland, College Park, including interviews with the National Turkey Federation; and Andrea Brown, who assisted me in looking up information at the National Agricultural Library as part of her summer internship with United Poultry Concerns a couple of years ago.

I am also grateful to A. R. Hogan of the Physicians Committee for Responsible Medicine and to the staff at People for the Ethical Treatment of Animals for sending me bundles of contemporary newspaper articles about everything from food poisoning to the growth of vegetarianism in America.

I am extremely grateful to Peter Singer for graciously reading my manuscript and for his generous endorsement of this book.

Finally, I would like to thank Martin Rowe for having chosen to publish my book and for his supreme and expert guidance in bringing it to life.

Introduction ~~~

MILTON, DORIS, AND SOME "TURKEYS" IN RECENT AMERICAN HISTORY

Nothing so unites us as gathering with one mind to murder someone we hate, unless it is coming together to share in a meal.—Margaret Visser, *The Rituals of Dinner*, 33

A tradition is a ritual that has come to represent an aspect of ourselves that we value.—Robin Marantz Hening, *USA Today*, November 25,1998

I DID NOT GROW UP AROUND TURKEYS. NOT UNTIL I was well into adulthood did I actually meet any that I can recall. My first encounter with turkeys took place at a farmed animal sanctuary in Avondale, Pennsylvania in the late 1980s when I went to work there one summer as a volunteer.[1] The turkeys I met at the sanctuary were not wild. They all derived from the meat industry. There was a flock of white turkey hens, about twenty, and two bronze turkeys, a male and a female named Milton and Doris. One of the things that impressed me then, and has stayed in my mind ever since, was the way the turkeys' voices, their "yelps," floated about the place in what seemed like an infinitely plaintive refrain. Another was how one or more of the hens would suddenly sit down beside me in the midst of my work, rigid and quivering, with her wings stiff and her head held high, awaiting my attention.

The faces of turkeys are fine-boned, and their eyes are large, dark, and almond-shaped. Doris, the bronze hen, wandered about the farm-yard all day by herself like an eternal embodiment of a "lost call," the call of a lost young turkey for its mother. She had a large, soft breast that felt sad to me whenever I picked her up. Milton, the bronze male turkey, followed me (and others) around on his gouty legs and swollen feet. His dark eyes watched us from inside a bristling armor of irides-cent brown feathers and pendant, heavily wrinkled pouches of folded head and facial skin of varying, shifting colors of emotion that to this day makes me think of a body with its soul imprisoned deep inside. Milton plodded behind people, stopping when they stopped, resuming his ponderous tread as they took up their feet again. He would stand before you, or appear unexpectedly at your back, manifesting himself almost scarily at times, decked out in his full array, his tail in a fabu-lous wheel, his wing ends dragging stiffly. Like the hens in their starched white wing skirts, crouched and quivering exactly where you were shoveling the muck, he awaited your response, and like them he would try, try again, patient and determined in his fixed agenda.

This, then, was my introduction to turkeys.

In 1998, a newspaper in Virginia announced that an interstate highway blocked by construction would no longer be a "turkey" (Messina, A1). Motorists heading home for the holidays could still get there in plenty of time for their Thanksgiving dinner. On a following page we see a photograph of a turkey on a table being touched by President Bill Clinton flanked by two other men with the caption, "Turkey has president to thank for its life" (AP, 1998).

A turkey dinner is simple in our society. Few people think about it. Likewise, the turkey as a metaphor of derision scarcely gets a thought from anyone. But the President of the United States "pardoning" a turkey? Is this turkey a malefactor? A criminal?

The view of animals as "innocent" or "guilty" has historical roots in Western society, although moral capability has almost always seemed to translate, in legal terms, into moral culpability in the case of animals. In European legal history, during the Middle Ages, animals were tried, convicted, and executed for killing humans. Pigs were frequently hanged. Laws in which animals were regarded as malefactors are set forth in Exodus 21, which prescribes that an ox that gores either a man or a woman shall be stoned to death, suggesting that bestiality was also a crime for which animals could be held liable and punished like humans (Wise, 25–31). Moral responsibility in animals was, and continues to be, a problem. Negatively speaking, a dog may be dangerous, but is it fair to refer to such a dog as "malicious"? In England, animals were not tried and convicted under penal law, as they were, for example, in France. However, horses, dogs, bears, and other animals were de facto accused of being idle and vicious and accordingly subjected to punishments such as baiting, hanging, and being locked up with a ram (Thomas, 97–98).

In the 17th century, following biblical precedent, the English Pilgrims and Puritans in Massachusetts executed both humans and nonhuman animals for bestiality. In 1679, for example, a woman and a dog were hanged together for allegedly committing the sexual act (Thomas, 98). In 1642, a teenaged servant named Thomas Granger was accused of conducting "buggery"—sexual intercourse—with a mare, a cow, two goats, five sheep, two calves, and a turkey (Bradford, 355–356).

Discovered raping the mare, Granger not only confessed to having sex with her then, "but sundry times before and at several times with all the rest of the forenamed in his indictment." He and a fellow sodomite insisted that sexual relations with animals was a custom "long used in old England."[2] Condemned by a jury, Granger was executed on September 8th. William Bradford, the Pilgrim governor of Plymouth Colony who conducted the execution, wrote:

A very sad spectacle it was. For first the mare and then the cow and the rest of the lesser cattle [cattle in the general sense of livestock, i.e., "live property"] were killed before his face, according to the law, Leviticus xx.15; and then he himself was executed. The cattle were all cast into a great and large pit that was digged of purpose for them, and no use made of any part of them. (Bradford, 356)

There is then in Western culture a history rooted in Scripture and beyond in which officialdom and nonhuman animals have come together in situations that attached guilt and maleficence to animals. Indeed, there is an entire history of scapegoating, ritual sacrifice, and demonization of animals in which animal victims have been placed in the position of bearing moral responsibility for the good or bad condition of society. Thus viewed, the presidential "pardoning" of a turkey is not so strange as it might first appear, nor is it a quirk of only our way of life. It may be an irony in the history of humankind and of our progress as a nation that we single out for mercy in a pardoning ceremony a member of a class whose sole purpose is to be slaughtered and eaten, a class that up to that very ceremonial moment has been fulfilling its purpose in slaughterhouses throughout America in preparation for the holiday ahead. The bird being pardoned by the President of the United States is being saved, paradoxically, both from and for the greater enjoyment of the Thanksgiving Day feast. The bird is an appetite teaser, with a load of symbolism surpassing the number of pounds it weighs. The pardoning ceremony accords with a sentimental holiday that is based on animal sacrifice.

In 1998, the same Virginia newspaper mentioned above lined up four "turkeys" in a row on a page and proceeded to "shoot" each of them from left to right (Turkeys, J1). The targets—Paula Jones, Linda Tripp, Saddam Hussein, and a turkey—were pictured from the neck up.[3] Their heads and the columns of text below each one suggested a live turkey shoot. The turkey shoot is an old sport based on the shooting of wild turkeys at roost in the trees. According to a writer in 1838, turkeys are "easily killed at roosts because the one being killed, the others sit fast." In 1947, it was said that "when turkeys are fired at on their roost, they only fly to the nearest tree so that all of them can be shot" (Schorger, 381). Thus a "turkey shoot" came to signify "a simple task or a helpless target"—a target "considered to be stupid and easy to catch" (Rawson, 394).

The last target in this virtual turkey shoot was mine. I asked, "Why do we celebrate with this hated bird?" and "Why do we hate this celebrated bird?" Turkey bashing is a routine part of America's Thanksgiving holiday celebration. Live turkey shoots are no longer commonly held, but virtual live turkey shoots continue to thrive in America's media culture. In the realm of rhetoric, Thanksgiving is open season on both turkeys and "turkeys." A question this book raises and seeks to answer is why.

---

1. Farm Sanctuary, 1988. See "A Peaceable Kingdom for Farm Animals (1989a)."
2. See Midas Dekkers, *Dearest Pet: On Bestiality* for an informative look at human sexual interest in and use of nonhuman animals through history to the present. Chapter 7, "God and Commandments," discusses the framing of laws and punishments for this class of offences in the Judeo-Christian tradition, and the "boom in bestiality trials from the sixteenth to the eighteenth centuries" (119). For further consideration of human sexual assault on other species, see Adams (1995b) and Beirne.
3. Federal employee Paula Jones charged President Bill Clinton with sexual harassment; federal employee Linda Tripp exposed an affair between President Clinton and White House aide Monica Lewinsky; Saddam Hussein is an elusive Iraqi despot.

A HISTORY OF IMAGE PROBLEMS

The Turkey as a Mock Figure of Speech and Symbol of Failure

> *I'm just like Job's turkey,*
> *I can't do nothing but gobble,*
> *I'm so poor, baby,*
> *I have to lean against the fence to gabble.*
> *Yeah, now, baby, I believe I'll change town,*
> *Lord, I'm so low down, baby,*
> *I declare I'm looking up at down....*
> —From a song by Big Bill Broonzy quoted in Studs Terkel,
> *Hard Times: An Oral History of the Great Depression,* 7

> *The Turkey 2000 Award: No contest*—Battlefield Earth.
> —Ella Taylor, *The Atlantic Monthly*, April 2001, 34

USE OF THE WORD *TURKEY* AS A SYNONYM FOR failure and worthlessness is not easy to trace, but it has a history. In *On Language*, William Safire writes:

For an explanation of the rampant use of the term turkey, for the old drip or jerk, let us turn to David Guralnik, editor of Webster's New World Dictionary: "'Turkey' is obviously a pejorative that is much in use, but its current provenance is uncertain. In earlier slang, it meant 'a coward.' It has also been used in the illicit drug trade for a fake capsule containing only sugar or chalk. And, of course, there's the theatrical use for a flop. Whether the current use retains some of these connotations or is a total reinvention based on the accepted stupidity of the bird is hard to say. Seems to me, I first heard it as a piece of black street slang." (181)

In 1984, Andrew Feinberg wrote in the *New York Times*, "By 1873, 'turkey' had come to mean an advantage or easy profit; soon it referred to someone who could be easily duped or caught. Since the Depression, the designation 'turkey' has been applied to more theatrical flops than any of us would care to remember." What's more,

> For those who believe that the turkey has been done a linguistic injustice, I've got some bad news: it's only getting worse. In the last 10 years, "turkey" has returned to vogue. The revival began as a sarcastic description of white people by blacks, according to Stuart Berg Flexner, author of "Listening to America." Now, it is entrenched as many people's insult of choice.

According to *Wicked Words*, students before and after 1945 used the term turkey to characterize an incompetent person who continually makes mistakes. Subsequently, turkey became a political byword for mockery of U. S. administration officials, which it still is. During the Carter administration (1977–81), Republicans joked, " 'Why does the president's staff always carry a frozen turkey aboard Air Force One?' Answer: 'Spare parts' " (Rawson, 394). In crime writer Ann Rule's 1983 novel *Possession*, the main character, a psychopathic killer, sizes up men who get in the way of the women he plots to possess as "turkeys." Watching a rival in one episode, the killer thinks to himself about how "[h]e would enjoy seeing the slow recognition on the Harley rider's face as he [the psychopath] unfolded his uniformed frame from the pickup, seeing the turkey's bravado seep out of his features when he realized who he'd been playing with" (94).

The word turkey as an all-purpose term of derision has been traced to the American theater. According to the Oxford English Dictionary, the earliest recorded use of the term comes from Walter Winchell. In "A Primer of Broadway Slang," in *Vanity Fair*, November 1927, Winchell distinguished between a flivver—"a synonym for a Ford car [that] was first used to describe a show that failed"—and a turkey, meaning "a third rate production" (132).

In 1939, Groucho Marx wrote a letter to a friend in which he complained that "[t]he boys at the studio have lined up another turkey for us...I saw the present one the other day and didn't much care for it" (OED).

Soon, anything that failed to live up to expectations or meet somebody's wishes was a "turkey." In James M. Cain's 1941 novel *Mildred Pierce*, a rock-studded beach unsuited to swimming is "simply a turkey," and a disliked law is a "turkey" as well (Wentworth and Flexner, 556).

Not surprisingly, Calvin Trillin's brief essay "The Case of the Purloined Turkey," alluding to Edgar Allen Poe's story "The Purloined Letter," is not really about the bird. Trillin lampoons a filched manuscript of a Richard Nixon book by contrasting the supposed excitement a journalist feels getting hold of such a prize before the world has seen it with the reality that the manuscript is full of platitudes and doesn't say anything interesting. "What," he asks, "is the purpose of being willing to reveal the contents of a purloined manuscript if there is nothing in it that bears revealing" (113)? In other words, what if the pilferer's treasure is just a....

During the 16th century, when turkeys first made their appearance in Europe, and a Turkish invasion of the European continent seemed possible, the word *Turk* became a stock term for a cruel, barbarous type of man and a pun for a type of exotic male savagery considered both ferocious and uproariously funny. In Rabelais's satiric 16th century novel *Gargantua and Pantagruel* (1552), the drunken Panurge regales banqueters with stories of how he "was almost roasted alive in Turkey but roasted a Turk on a spit instead" (Bakhtin, 332). Interestingly, the word turk comes from the Gaelic word "torc," meaning a wild boar (Wentworth and Flexner, 556). Thereafter, the word underwent some startling metamorphoses.

In America, the word turkey was used by the Irish and others to signify an Irish immigrant in the United States. In James T. Farrell's 1932 novel, *Young Lonigan*, the character Dooley is "one comical turkey, funnier than anything you'd find in real life" (OED). According to *Wicked Words*,

> The Turk as Irisher, dated to 1914, sometimes is confused with the well-known bird: "Terrible Turkey McGovern, ah, there was a sweet fighting harp for you, a real fighting turkey with dynamite in each mitt...." (James T. Farrell, *Young Lonigan*, 1932 quoted in Rawson, 394)

Here a ferocious mammal, the wild boar, has been transformed through the vagaries of discourse and cultural mishmash into a barbarous fellow, a comical figure, a musical instrument, and a very strange bird, a mélange that continues to this day. Several years ago, the *Washington Post* published a "field guide" to the various "turkeys" one was likely to meet on the plane ride home for Thanksgiving—people ranging from obnoxious strangers to insufferable acquaintances to you yourself—"if you're thinking your companion is a turkey, he probably sees a gobbler when he looks at you too" (Curcio).

Gobbler, the Yankee term for a male turkey, comprises age-old echoes of jabber, chatter, babble, and gabble. *Gobble* is an all-purpose word for noisy nonsense talk and voracious ill-mannered swallowing—greed (Webster's). *Turkey-cock* is a epithet for the absurdly arrogant pompous boasting type of man, based on the male turkey's strut and gobble during the mating season combined with stock images of the barbarous Turk (Webster's).

The term *Gobbledygook*, dating to World War II, is attributed to a U.S. House Representative from Texas, Maury Maverick, who, as chairman of the Smaller War Plants Corp, denounced the bureaucratic jargon at the meetings he attended—"maladjustments co-extensive with problem areas," and so on—the kind of language George Orwell blasted in his classic essay, "The Politics of the English Language."

Tired of the malarkey, Maverick issued an order on March 30, 1944, banning "gobbledygook language." He warned: "Be short and say what you're talking about....No more patterns, effectuating, dynamics. Anyone using the words activation or implementation will be shot." Asked where he got the term, Maverick told the *New York Times Magazine* (May 21, 1944): "People ask me where I got gobbledygook. I do not know. It must have come in a vision. Perhaps I was thinking of the old bearded turkey gobbler back in Texas who was always gobbledy-gobbling and strutting with ludicrous pomposity. At the end of this gobble there was a sort of gook" (Rawson, 174).

Maverick may well have heard echoes of another time and place. The Scottish term *bubbly-jock*, which more or less rhymes with turkey-cock, similarly ridicules noisy displays of vanity. Rival regiments nick-named the Royal Scots Greys the Bubbly Jocks (Green, 120). In his biography of Frederick the Great (1865), Thomas Carlyle cries out against deference to the scribbling dunces of false culture, "Oh my winged Voltaire, to what dunghill Bubbly-Jocks you do stoop with homage" (OED).

I first encountered *bubbly-jock* in a book published in 1844 by William Howitt, *The Rural Life of England*. Lamenting the cankerous envy rampant among the gentry, Howitt writes,

[I]t would be giving a most one-sided view of the rural
life of the rich, if we left it to be inferred that "the trail
of the serpent" was not to be perceived at times on the
fair lawns, and up the marble steps of rural palaces;
that the great "Bubbly-Jock" (Turkey-Cock), which
[Walter] Scott contended that every man found in his
path, did not shew himself there. The Serpent and the
Bubbly-Jock which disturb and poison the rural life of
the educated classes in England, are the very same
which dash with bitter all English society in the same
classes. They are the pride of life, and the pride of the
eye. They are the continual struggle for precedence,
and those jealousies which are generated by a false
social system. Every man lives now-a-day for public
observation. (78)

Bubbly-jock has been traced to the 18th century, though quite likely it arose much earlier in popular speech when turkeys first began
appearing in Scotland in the 16th century. It is likely that the turkey
got tagged with a name already in use to describe rustics with runny
noses. Bubbly-jock comprises two words: *bubbly*, meaning snotty—
dirty with nose mucus—as in "a bubbly bairn" (child); hence, tearful,
blubbering, sniveling; and *Jock*, or Jack, designating a rustic, peasant,
or farmer in the old-fashioned sense of a boorish or incompetent fellow
(Webster's). Eighteenth-century sources speculated that "bubbly" could
have derived from the shape of the turkey's wattle, or dewlap, the fold
of loose red skin that hangs from a turkey's throat, which, it was said,
has "considerable resemblance to the snot collected at a dirty child's
nose": "His nose was like a bublie-cocks neb" (1779). In the North of
England *snotergob* was a name given to "the red part of a turkey's head,"
according to the Scottish National Dictionary.

"Bubbly" might also be an imitation of the male turkey's gobble, but why limit the origin one way or the other? The turkey has a "bubbly" head—"bare, rough, warty," according to Grzimek (19)—as well as a bubbly-sounding gobble, inviting a synesthetic response. The gobble has been mimetically characterized as sounding like "gil-obble, obble, obble, quit, quit, cut," and "gil-obble-obble-obble" (Schorger, 247), and the scantily feathered head and upper part of the bird's neck have skin bumps of various sizes called caruncles that are particularly prominent on the adult male bird's head (Dickson, 32).

A 16th-century admirer raved over the male turkey's "bubbles" as well as his amazing colors:

> The colour of that wrinkled skinne about his head (which hangeth ouer his byll and about his necke, al swelling as it were with little blathers) he changeth from time to time like the Chamaelon, to al colours of the Rainebowe, sometimes white, sometimes red, sometimes blewe, sometimes yellowe, which colours euer altring, the byrd appearth as it were a myracle of nature (Barnaby Googe [1577] quoted in Schorger, 103).

The turkey's chameleonic quality—the bird's ability to change skin colors rapidly as a reflection of changing moods the way certain lizards do—is a reminder of the ancestral relationship between birds and reptiles in the history of evolution. Fossil records in the Southwestern United States and Mexico show the turkey going back at least as far as the late Pliocene epoch, between two and five million years ago, before the time of the glaciers (Dickson, 7). A number of extinct species have been identified, although much like the ostrich and the emu, large flightless fowl believed to have branched off from the main line of avian evolution eighty or ninety million years ago (Dawson and Herd, 41), the turkey poses the prospect of even greater antiquity. Naturalist Joe

Hutto, who raised and lived with mechanically incubated wild turkeys, suggests in his book *Illumination in the Flatwoods: A Season with the Wild Turkey* that the turkey could be in fact "a twenty-million-year-old bird" (120).

As a mock figure of speech, the turkey is remarkable for the range of anthropomorphic roles it has been assigned, a rather odd fact considering the bird's singular appearance, its conspicuous one-of-a-kindness. In the history of avian nomenclature and species identification, the turkey has borne a burden of confusion that in many ways is just as remarkable, and strangely parallel. To this we now turn.

2 ⁓

THE TURKEY BY MANY OTHER NAMES

Confusing Nomenclature and Species Identification Surrounding the Native American Bird

> *The nomenclature of the turkey has followed a torturous path....Long thought to have been of Asiatic or African origin, it received extremely inappropriate common and scientific names.*—A. W. Schorger, *The Wild Turkey: Its History and Domestication*, 72, 3

> *The pheasants of the Old World correspond to the TURKEYS... of America.*—*Grzimek's Animal Life Encyclopedia*, 19

T HE TURKEY WAS LONG HELD TO BELONG TO THE family of birds known as pheasants, *Phasianidae*, which includes among other birds the chicken (jungle fowl), the peafowl, the quail, and the guinea fowl.[1] A common feature of these birds is that they are not native to Europe, although the question of any species's ultimate origin poses a challenge. Native Americans, for example, are not literally natives of America. They crossed the Bering Strait from Siberia to America 25,000 to 40,000 years ago (Irwin, 5). Like people, birds and other animals have migrated or been shifted in the course of millennia around the globe. By the time the Europeans first saw the turkey, the peafowl, and the guinea fowl, each of these pheasant-like birds had long been established in a particular part of the world and could thus be regarded as native to it: the peafowl in Asia, the guinea fowl in Africa, the turkey in North America. Where any of these birds "began," and under what circumstances they came to resemble or differ from one another, is not well known. Not until the 1930s, for example, was the Congo Peacock determined to be a native of Africa, upsetting the former notion that pheasants came exclusively from Asia or India (Drimmer, 988–989).

To this day, it is uncertain how close turkeys are to pheasants. To date, no turkey fossil remains have been reported in Asia, and no Asian pheasant fossil remains have been identified in North America. A 200-year effort to label these birds has had little success. In 1758, Linnaeus classified the turkey as *Meleagris gallopavo*, although the genus *meleagris* is the Greco-Roman name for the African guinea fowl,[2] and the species name *gallopavo* is the Latin word for the peafowl of Asia: *gallus* for cock or rooster; *pavo* for peacock. Terminologically, *Meleagris gallopavo* is a guinea fowl–chickenlike peacock, of which there are five recognized wild subspecies: the eastern wild turkey (*M.g. silvestris*); Florida wild turkey (*M.g. osceola*); Merriam's wild turkey of the mountains of the western United States (*M.g. merriami*); the Rio Grande wild turkey of the south central plains states and northeastern Mexico (*M.g. intermedia*); and Gould's wild turkey of northwestern Mexico and parts of southern Arizona and New Mexico (*M.g. mexicana*). The accepted forerunner of the domestic turkey, *M.g. gallopavo* of southern Mexico, is believed to be extinct (See Dickson, 6–7 and color photo section).

Pheasants and pheasant-like birds, including the turkey, belong to the order known as *galliforms*, meaning cock-shaped (Dickson, 18). Galliforms make their nests on the ground rather than in trees like robins or blue jays, or on cliff ledges as do penguins, gulls, terns, doves, and some pelicans. Galliforms include chickens, turkeys, pheasants, quails, peafowl, guinea fowl, and a host of other birds that were often confused with the turkey. In Ireland and Scotland into the late 18th century, a large grouse known as the capercaillie was still being referred to in places as a "wild turkey" (Schorger, 4).

Previously, galliforms were considered primitive birds, not only in the sense of very old, but mentally low as well. As summarized in 1918: "Considering the group as a whole, the Galliformes, or fowl-like birds, are unquestionably low in the scale of avian evolution. In spite of their fine feathers and elaborately specialized plumage characters, neither anatomically nor mentally are they of high rank" (Beebe, quoted in Schorger, 70). Today this view is no longer tenable, as will be seen in the chapter on the turkey's intelligence.

Meanwhile, various methods were tried in the 1940s and the 1950s in an effort to disentangle the taxonomies of the turkey, guinea fowl, peafowl, and the chicken, a project that proved largely chimerical. It is almost as if these birds, prevented from escaping us on a physical level, have thus far succeeded in eluding our grasp on a more esoteric plane. Electrophoretic examination based on the separation of particles in fluids of egg white proteins from several different species indicated that the turkey was closer to the chicken than to the guinea fowl or the pheasant. The same method led other researchers to conclude that the guinea fowl was closer to the peafowl than to the turkey, and that the three species showed a clearer relationship to one another than to the pheasant. In the 1950s, immunology and chromatography suggested that the turkey and the guinea fowl are more closely related to each other than to the chicken. Electrophoretic patterns identified in the 1950s indicated that the turkey is a pheasant. On the basis of immunology, a researcher concluded in 1959 that the pheasant, the guinea fowl, and the turkey are closely related, while the chicken and the quail, "which belong with *Phasianus* to the same family, are rather remote from one another, and from all other species" (Schorger, 71–72).

The word *turkey* entered the European vernacular during the Middle Ages. The best explanation is that the Turkish Empire was the main European trade route to the East through which exotic birds such as the peafowl, a gorgeous pheasant, were transported to the European continent in trade. In the Middle Ages, nearly everything exotic was obtained in or through Turkey or Arabia (Schorger, 16). Three centuries before any actual turkeys appeared in 16th-century Europe, the word *turkey* was being used to describe exotic birds from Asia. According to A. W. Schorger in *The Wild Turkey: Its History and Domestication*, "Any large bird that spread its tail was a peafowl, or a turkey" (3).

Even after it became generally known that the turkey was an American bird, the idea clung that the turkey came from Turkey. Samuel Johnson defined the bird in 1755 as "[a] large domestick fowl brought from Turkey" (Schorger, 16). As late as 1847, Walter Dickson declared that "[t]he name of the Turkey alludes to the resemblance between the head of the Turkey cock, and the helmet of a Turkish soldier, which, as represented in old drawings, appears formally to have consisted of a bluish-coloured coat of mail over his head and shoulders with red lappets" (Feltwell, 16).

As noted, the genus name for the turkey is *Meleagris*, which is Greek and Latin for guinea fowl. For two centuries, the turkey was confused not only with the peafowl from Asia, but with the guinea fowl from Africa. In 1552, Sir Thomas Elyot talked about "Meleagrides, birdes, which we doo call hennes of Genny or Turkie henne" (Schorger, 4); and an English recipe for boiled poultry published in 1615 refers to guinea fowl as "young turkeys" (Markham, 79, 259). Such confusion reflected the fact that in the 16th century, when the turkey was imported from America, the guinea fowl was imported into the Spanish dominions from Africa through Turkey (Drimmer, 994).

It has been suggested that the name *turkey* echoes the turkey's call notes, *turk, turk, turk*, or that it may be a mispronunciation of aboriginal Mexican Indian names for the turkey: *huexolotl, tou, totoli, tulu, tutk, tunuk* (Schorger, 16–18). The name could have come from the Hebrew word *tukki*, meaning "peacock," a plausible choice given that Jewish poultry merchants in the Middle East were prominent in bringing the peafowl to Europe (Dickson, 6). Other possible derivations

include the Hindustani *taus* and the Malabar *togei*—both words meaning peafowl in the trade ports of western India (Schorger, 16). Given
the exotic mystique that surrounded the word *turkey* well into the 18th
century, Schorger's view of Benjamin Franklin's 1784 letter to his
daughter, Sarah Bache, in which Franklin vouched that the turkey
would have made a better national seal than the bald eagle, may be true
(Bigelow, 279–280). "It would have been highly incongruous,"
Schorger writes, "to have selected a bird with so foreign a name as
turkey" as our national seal (16).

As early as 1498, Petrus Alonsus, voyaging along the Venezuelan
coast, saw "[i]n their woodes...innumerable Peacockes, nothing unlyke
oures, saving that the males differ litle from the females" (Wright, 344).
The birds he saw were not peacocks, however. They may have been
turkeys, or perhaps curassows, crested birds that are similar in size to
small turkeys.

Descriptions by the historian Peter Martyr (Pietro Martire), secretary to the Council of the Indies in the 16th century, are likewise
uncertain because of the then prevailing confusion of Old and New
World birds. In 1516, Martyr wrote that South Americans gave to
members of a Spanish expedition "a great multitude of theyr peacockes, both cockes and hennes, deade and alyve, as well to satisfie theyr
present necessitie, as also to cary with theym into Spayne for encrease"
(Wright, 344). Several year later (1530), he described what he thought
were, and could very well have been, turkeys:

> The Mexicans raise this bird (*pauonum*) as chickens
> (*gallinas*) are raised in Spain. Turkeys resemble peafowl
> in size and in the color of their plumage. The females
> lay from twenty to thirty eggs. The males are always in
> rut so that their flesh is indifferent. Like peacocks they
> display before the females, spreading the tail in the
> form of a wheel. They parade before them, take four or

more steps, then shiver as if affected with a strong fever.
On the neck are displayed feathers of various colors,...sometimes blue, green, or purplish according to
the movement of the feathers. (Schorger, 12–13)

These sound like turkeys, particularly the part about the spreading
of the tail in the form of a wheel, except that all of the turkeys known
today have bare or nearly bare necks, and changes of color appear in the
skin rather than in the bird's feathers. Still, a desiccated thousand-year-
old turkey found in the Tularosa Cave in New Mexico in 1905 showed
a densely feathered neck to the base of the skull, making it possible that
Martyr's turkey was a type that no longer exists (Schorger, 1961, 138).
Quite possibly, Martyr's turkey is a composite of contemporary Spanish
descriptions of turkeys, peacocks, and similar kinds of birds. Despite
the confusion, documents show that turkeys were being sent to Spain
for propagation by royal decree by 1511 (Schorger, 9).

The Spanish had many names for the turkey. The terms *gallina,*
gallus, and *pavo* ("hen," "cock," and "peacock") were adapted from the
chicken, a native of Southeast Asia long known and raised in Spain and
unknown in the New World prior to Columbus (Schorger, 17). These
names were applied not only to turkeys but to the curassow, crested
guan, horned guan, chachalacas, and the ocellated turkey of the
Yucatan Peninsula of southeastern Mexico. The ocellated turkey is
classed as a separate species of turkey, *Meleagris ocellata,* a bird who
whistles instead of gobbling or clucking, and whose tail coverts have
eyespots similar to those of a peacock. The Indians never succeeded in
domesticating the ocellated turkey, of whom it has been said that the
bird "flies with the greatest rapidity at the sight of man, regardless of
distance" (Schorger, 68). This beautiful wild turkey with blue-green
feathers lives in the Yucatan region of southern Mexico, Belize, and
northern Guatemala (Dickson, 7, 19, 45). In his book *Autobiography*
of a Bird-Lover, ornithologist Frank Chapman describes shooting an

ocellated turkey in Mexico and a failed attempt to get live specimens from there to Paris in the late 19th century (145–149).

Based on primary sources—narratives, histories, memoirs, and letters—Schorger says that "the *gallina* ['hen,' 'chicken' or 'fowl'] of the Spaniards in the Western world was the turkey" (17), and that *pavo* (peacock) was probably the most prevalent Spanish name for the turkey in 16th-century Mexico (18). Gomara's *La Historia General de la Indias* (1554) cites *gallipavo* as a popular Spanish name for the turkey in Cuba, and Rodrigo Ranjel, writing about the De Soto expedition that started north from Cuba in 1539, says that the party breakfasted on turkeys, called *guanaxas*. Other Spanish names for the turkey in Central America and Mexico in the 16th century included *gallo de papada* ("chicken cock with a throat wattle"), *pavo de la papada* ("peacock with a throat wattle"), and *gallina por barba* ("chicken with a beard"). In the late 17th century, Gemelli-Careri referred to turkeys in Mexico as *guaxalote, galli d'India, galli d'India silvestri,* and *gallo de la tierra* (Schorger, 17). The frequently cited "chickens of India" or "chickens of the Indias" recalls the fact that the Spanish fleet, led by the Italian navigator Christopher Columbus in 1492, originally set sail for, and believed they had landed in, India in their search for spices and gold.

Columbus and his crew may have been the first Europeans ever to see a turkey, but no one knows (Schorger, 4). When they landed at Cabo de Honduras on August 14, 1502 on Columbus's fourth voyage, the native inhabitants served them *gallinas de la tierra,* "native fowls" or "chickens of the country." Henceforth, turkeys were called by this name in numerous expedition records. One thing is certain. Turkeys were abundant in the Americas in the 16th century. The "India" the Europeans landed in was teeming with turkeys both wild and domestic.

---

1. The guinea fowl is now usually grouped in the family *Numididae,* formerly and debatably a genus or subfamily of *Phasianidae* (*Webster's*).

2. In classical mythology the sisters of Meleagros were turned into guinea fowl whose plumage beads became the tears they shed over their brother's death. The story in Homer's *Iliad* (Schorger, 72) is retold in Ovid's *Metamorphoses.*

3 ⁓

A TRUE ORIGINAL NATIVE OF AMERICA

A true original native of America.—Benjamin Franklin, letter
to his daughter Sarah Bach

URKEYS WERE AN INTEGRAL PART OF THE NATIVE
American cultures and continental landscape encountered by
the Europeans. Turkeys occupied North, South, and Central
America, the West Indies, and Mexico. They roamed throughout the
oak-hickory and northern hardwood forests of the northeastern United
States from the New England seacoasts to southern Ontario. They
ranged from Pennsylvania and Ohio into the Midwestern prairies and
the Great Plains, and south from Maryland through coastal Virginia,
along the southeastern regions of the country and into Florida, where
they lived along the wooded streams. Turkeys were numerous in the
Ohio Valley and in the southwestern regions of what would become
Oklahoma, Texas, New Mexico, Arizona, and Southern California. Their
ancestral homes included the Ponderosa pine forests of Arizona, the
Yucatan Peninsula of southeastern Mexico, the Rio Grande of the south-
central plains, and the Chesapeake Bay area of the Mid-Atlantic states.
Only in the coldest climates of the Western Hemisphere were turkeys sel-
dom or never seen—the Pacific Northwest, the high mountain ranges of
the Appalachians, the Adirondacks in New York, northern Canada.

Although the eastern Indians hunted and made use of wild turkeys, they did not domesticate them as did the Pueblo Indians of the Southwest, the Aztecs, the Mayans, and other pre-Columbian inhabitants of Mexico and Central America. In such places, turkeys had been domesticated—procured in the wild, propagated, raised, and restrained—for a thousand years for food, feathers, and sacrificial purposes, including live burial. For example, three hundred desiccated adult turkeys discovered at a site in Tseahatso, Arizona, and dated at 400–700 C.E., are believed to have been used for food and feather production (Breitburg, 156). According to Breitburg, "the intensive nature of Mexican turkey production could very well have accommodated the fabulous quantities of live birds and feathers needed to meet the demands for tribute payments and festive occasions" (170).

Use of Turkeys in Mesoamerica: Mexico and Central America

Wild turkeys living in the Sierras were caught and raised by the Mexican Tarahumaras, a Taracahitian people of southern Sonora and Chihuahua, who also stole wild turkey eggs and placed them under their own brooding hens. At night, the turkeys slept on top of their houses and in nearby trees. According to reports, they were so tame it was not necessary to clip their wings (Schorger, 140). The Tarahumaras were said to have a turkey dance and to use wild turkeys in sacrificial feasts. At one of their burial sites, a human body was recovered with a wad of cotton between the legs mixed with blue jay, woodpecker, and turkey feathers (Schorger, 364). In his *General History of the Things of New Spain* (c. 1570), the Spanish writer Sahagun described the wild turkey hens (*gallinas monteses*) and turkey cocks he observed in the forests of Mexico in 1529 (Schorger, 14).

When Cortes and his men entered Mexico in 1519, they found domesticated turkeys throughout the Aztec Empire. Aztec ambassadors offered them turkeys, humans, cherries, and maize bread to eat, and people were seen carrying turkeys at the Port of San Juan de Ulua

(Schorger, 9–10). Turkeys were in every town. The Mexican markets were full of them. When Cortes marched into the city of Mexico, he wrote in 1520, "[t]here is a street for game in which are sold all kinds of native birds such as turkeys, partridges, quails, [and] wild ducks" (Schorger, 12). Diaz, who was with him, said they sold *gallinas* and *gallos de papada* (turkey hens and cocks). Others reported huge numbers of eggs from turkeys, geese, and many other birds in the markets of Mexico. A turkey was exchanged for a bundle of maize; one turkey was said to be worth three or four Spanish chickens. Cooked turkeys were sold as well as live ones. At certain festivals an entire turkey was served in a tamale (minced meat and red peppers rolled in corn meal) wrapped in palm leaves (Schorger, 12).

Aztec families raised turkeys for food along with a hairless type of dog. The turkeys lived in the garden next to the house and in special poultry-runs. At meals, according to Sahagun, "the turkey-meat was put on top [of the dish], and the dog underneath, to make it seem more" (Soustelle, 128, 152).

While poor people ate turkeys only on special occasions, and the average family ate its own birds or shopped at the market, the Aztec emperor's royal household and the lords of the states and towns consumed huge numbers of turkeys exacted as tribute from the communities they ruled. In 1430, the lord of Texcoco required one hundred turkeys daily, or 36,500 turkeys a year. Everyone in the town of Misquiahuala had to give to the Aztec emperor Montezuma one turkey every twenty days. In 1519, this town of 7,500 people would have contributed to the emperor 135,000 turkeys, or at least 54,000 turkeys if only the adults were counted. In some towns, such as Tepeucila, only the lords were allowed to eat turkeys (Schorger, 10).

Montezuma's mealtimes are described in the following account of the war chief's turkey tributes. Kitchens and storehouses occupied much space in Montezuma's household,

for not only were there some three hundred guests
served at each meal but also a thousand guards and
attendants. In contrast to the profusion within, outside
the kitchen door squatted patiently a threadbare group
of countrymen from whose carrying bags swayed the
mottled heads of the trussed turkeys [skewered or
bound by the wings for cooking] which they had
brought as offerings for the royal larder. (Vaillant, 231)

The number of turkeys required for each lord for the fiesta of the
Tlaxcalan god Camaxtli was 1,400 to 1,600 daily (Schorger, 10). At
one Mexican feast, between 1,000 and 1,500 turkeys were reported
consumed (11). In addition to human consumption and use of feathers, huge numbers of turkeys were demanded for Montezuma's captive
raptors and mammalian carnivores. The raptors alone got 500 turkeys
each day, including a turkey a day for each large eagle. According to
Cortes and Motolinia, Montezuma's raptors ate nothing but turkeys,
while the mammalian carnivores were thrown turkeys, dogs, and deer.
Schorger speculates that "[b]etween Montezuma's menagerie and his
large household, it seems safe to assume that his levy was one thousand
turkeys per day, or 365,000 yearly." When Cortes requested an estate
from Montezuma, he received in the bargain fifteen hundred turkeys,
some for breeding, others for food (11).

Turkeys were ritually sacrificed in Mexico. In Central Mexico, a
young turkey hen's bones were recovered at an altar in the city of
Oaxaca (Breitburg,156). The Mayans of southeastern Mexico and
Central America held a *cutz-cal-tzo*, a "ritual strangling of turkeys during the fiesta of the patron saint of Dzitas" (Schorger, 365). The
Mayans sacrificed and beheaded turkey hens as part of their feasts for
the gods that controlled the earth's waters. Believing the bird symbol-
ized the south, the Mayans sacrificed turkeys to their god of the south,
Nohol. According to Roger Caras in *A Perfect Harmony*, the Mayans'

descendants today "still forecast the weather by observing turkey behavior. If the birds take dust baths, they believe rain is coming" (Caras, 204).

The Zapotec people of central Mexico sprinkled turkey blood on their newly planted fields. In Mexico and Central America, as in the Southwest, turkeys were regarded as symbolic manifestations of earth, rain, and fertility, and were ritually sacrificed to manipulate these elements (Breitburg, 168).

At Casas Grandes, a trade outpost in northwestern Mexico linking the Southwest and Central America to Mexico in the 13th, 14th, and 15th centuries, turkeys apparently were not eaten, which may have been taboo. It is believed that Casas Grandes kept a large turkey population for sacrifice, ritual burial, feather production, trade, and the tribute demanded by territorial Mexican rulers. There were turkey roosting pens and holding areas as well as a place for breeding and maintaining turkeys. Based on site remains, "Casas Grandes turkeys appear to have been a highly admixed population of birds bred at the site and acquired from settlements throughout the Southwest" (Breitburg, 160).

Use of Turkeys in the Southwest

Archeology indicates that turkeys were domesticated in the Southwest sometime between 700 and 1100 C.E., though they were being used as far back as 200 C.E. or even earlier (Schorger, 20–21). Turkeys were taken from the Ponderosa pine forests and elsewhere, and penned or kept in caves by the cliff-dwelling Pueblo people. Caves containing ancient turkey droppings, desiccated adult and young turkeys, turkey eggs, and loose and tied turkey feathers have been identified, and artifacts of turkey bones, beads, and bird callers have been found in these caves. Burial-site recovery of complete turkey skeletons with missing heads, sometimes in association with human burial, indicates sacrificial use of the birds, and most recovered bone awls (small, pointed tools for making holes in leather and wood) are made of turkey bones. An ancient wall in New Mexico contained turkey leg bones and gravel from the turkey's gizzard mixed with the mortar (Schorger, 33–35). The Spanish reported that the pueblos typically had large flocks of turkeys. In the southern Piro pueblos, for instance, "each Indian had his own turkey corral holding 100 birds" (Schroeder, 99).

Spanish records of the 16th-century Southwest emphasize the use of feathers over the birds' use as food; however, some of the pueblos were said to make corn flour gruel (*atoles*) with turkey and buffalo meat (Schroeder, 99). Someone later wrote that the Indians of the Southwest with whom he ate would kill a wild turkey, bleed, eviscerate, and slightly pluck the bird, then cook it on hot coals, a method imitated by white people who roasted fully feathered turkeys in a hole in the ground (Schorger, 370). The Zuni told Coronado that they did not eat turkeys but kept them "merely for the sake of procuring the feathers." At Cibola, New Mexico, one of Coronado's men wrote, "For food they have an abundance of maize...[and] some turkeys like those of Mexico, which they keep more for their feathers than for eating as they make robes of them since they do not have cotton" (34).

The Espejo expedition of 1583 reported that the inhabitants of Hawikuh, in New Mexico, presented them with tortillas, turkeys, and rabbits. In 1598, these people were said to offer turkey feathers to their idols (Schorger, 34), fitting the overall pattern of using turkey feathers for religious purposes as well as for clothing and ornaments throughout the Southwest.

Regarding the religious symbolism of turkeys among the Pueblo Indians, Schorger writes, "The turkey is mentioned in the Zuni cosmogenic legend, and its tail-feather markings are said to be caused by the slime of the earlier wet world. It is a sacred bird....The feathers were believed capable of bringing rain. There is also a legend that the turkey, in trying to raise the sun, had the feathers of its head burned off; hence, the head is red and bare" (362).

The Pueblo Indians made prayer sticks, masks, and headdresses out of turkey feathers. As a result of live plucking for these purposes, the turkeys in the Hopi villages were said to have a "ragged aspect." Among the Hopis, feathers from the short layer in the turkey tail were put on the backs of two prayer sticks tied together to represent male and female. The feathers were supposed to keep the symbolic figures warm. Feathers were also used to make prayer plumes, and bristles from the beard of the turkey (a tuft of coarse black hairs that grows in the breast of adult male turkeys and some females) were added to the feathers of some Hopi prayer sticks (Schorger, 362). The Rodriguez-Chamuscado expedition of 1581–82 noted that a pueblo in the Galisteo Basin had "sticks adorned with plumes which a dancer who had been lashed gave to the spectator Indians so that they could place them in the fields and in pools of water to bring rain" (Schroeder, 99). In general, according to Schroeder, "the Pueblo land was said to be plentiful with native turkeys, and the people had the practice of worshipping with feathers and offerings of almost everything, including birds" (100).

In addition to religious use, turkey feathers were used to make clothes, blankets, pouches, costume ornaments, and necklaces (Schorger, 360). The Piros raised turkeys and made turkey feather quilts both for sleeping and for wearing as cloaks (Schroeder, 99). Zia women wore turkey feather blankets over their dresses, and at Acoma "the dance-women wore 'Mexican blankets' (cotton) with paintings, feathers, and other trappings." Turkey feather robes were reported at Pecos in a journal kept during the de Sosa expedition of 1590–91 (100).

The making of turkey feather fabrics consisted of stripping the large wing and tail feathers from live turkeys, wrapping the feathers around feather cords, and weaving the cords into robes and blankets (Schorger, 360). Breitburg cites the use of live birds as a dominant motive for domesticating them: "With human expansion, greater importance was attached to procuring live birds, adapting them to settlement life, allowing them to breed, and providing the required assistance to sustain growing populations. Humans because of their particular needs continued to favor live turkeys as a source of ritual feathers, for sacrifice, and in the production of textiles" (168).

Use of Turkeys by the Eastern Woodland Indians

Though abundant, turkeys were not tamed by Indians in the eastern United States and south central and southeastern Canada. Wild turkey poults and eggs were stolen, but turkeys were not kept as they were in the Southwest, Mexico, and Central America (Schorger, 137). There are no references by the English, Dutch, and French colonists and their predecessors to the raising of turkeys by the tribal cultures on the eastern seaboard and further west. These cultures included the Algonquian peoples who occupied land from Labrador to the Great Plains and from New England to the Mid-Atlantic regions; the Iroquois tribes in New York, Quebec, and Ontario; and the Muskogean tribes of southern Mississippi, Alabama, Georgia, and Louisiana.

In general, these groups consisted of semi-nomadic hunters, gatherers, and agriculturalists who lived in permanent villages in which they raised and prepared corn, beans, squash, and other edible plants, as well as gathering nuts and berries. Hunting and fishing were primary food-gathering occupations.

The Eastern woodland Indians hunted virtually every animal in sight, including the turkey. They hunted turkeys with bows and arrows made of turkey feathers, bones, and spurs. These bow and arrow hunters were poor long-range shooters whose skill consisted, rather, in silently stalking and tracking wounded animals over long distances (Irwin, 25). Turkeys were lured by callers made of turkey wing bones, and the heads, skins, and tail feathers of turkeys were used as decoys to attract live turkeys in order to kill them. Indians could imitate the call of a turkey poult for its mother, and the male's gobble could be imitated perfectly. Hunters would hide behind a log and mimic his voice.

When a bird approached, they "raised the spread tail of a turkey above the log and moved it like a strutting bird" (Schorger, 380).

Other Indian hunting methods described in Schorger included circular hunts, use of snares and nets, driving the birds into pens and trees, catching them with baited hooks, and use of blowguns. Driving turkey flocks into trees was a common practice. Chased on foot, and later on galloping horses, wild turkeys were driven at top speed accompanied by "yelling and making as much noise as possible to force them into trees from which they were shot" (Schorger, 377–379).

Similar methods were used in the Southwest, including turkey-call imitations by Indians hiding behind a rock, a tree, or a log. In Texas, the Tonkawa Indians ran turkeys down on horseback (Schorger, 222), and 20th-century Apaches would "have a party flush the turkeys from one bank of a stream toward another party stationed about one-half mile distant from the opposite bank where the birds were expected to alight." The turkeys were then "shot with arrows or clubbed" (381).

As for bone-tube callers to lure turkeys and other birds, Schorger says this tool is probably the oldest and most widely used, as indicated by archeological sites from the Atlantic to the Pacific. The tone produced resembles "that of a mother turkey calling its young." Indeed, it is "an easy matter to imitate all of the calls of the wild turkey" (396).

Methods employed by the Indians to lure, trap, and kill turkeys were so numerous it is not surprising to learn that Cherokee and Chickasaw boys made blowguns especially to shoot turkeys in the eyes. These weapons consisted of slender arrows about a foot long made of cane, prepared so as to fit into wider cane tubes seven to ten feet long. They were plugged with thistledown at one end and puffed on at the other end. A turkey could be killed with a blowgun from thirty to forty feet away if the head was hit, although these weapons were said to be "generally defective in straightness" (Schorger, 379).

Powhatans' Use of the Turkey

To get an idea of the role of turkeys in a particular tribe of eastern wood-land Indians, let us look at the Powhatan of Virginia. The Powhatans were one of the Algonquian-speaking groups of Indians encountered by the Jamestown colonists along the Virginia coast in 1607. As Helen C. Rountree states in *The Powhatan Indians of Virginia: Their Traditional Culture,* "The premier game bird on land was (and still is) the wild turkey" (28). The Powhatans hunted turkeys and other land fowl with dogs. They lured turkeys with callers made of turkey wing bones and shot them with bows and arrows. These forty-five-inch-long arrows were "fletched with turkey feathers cut to shape with a sharpened reed knife." The Powhatans did not tame or form companionships with animals, according to Rountree. They hunted intensively and are not on record as showing any fear of punishment by animal powers for over-hunting (40–42).

The Powhatans ate well. The following description by English colonists in 1612 puts the turkey in a context of consumption practiced by the Powhatans throughout the year:

> In March and April they live much vpon their [fishing] Weeres, and feed on Fish, Turkeys, and Squirrells and then as also sometymes in May [John Smith adds: "and June"] and June they plant their Feilds and sett their Corne, and live after those Monethes mostly off Acrons, Wallnutts, Chesnutts, Chechinquamyns and Fish, but to mend their dyett, some disperse themselves in smale Companies, and live vpon such beasts as they can kill, with their bowes and arrowes. Vpon Crabbs, Oysters, Land Tortoyses, Strawberries, Mulberries and such like; In June, July, and August they feed vpon the rootes of Tockohowberryes [wild potatoes], Grownd-nuts, Fish, and greene Wheat [corn], and sometyme

vpon a kynd of Serpent, or great snake of which our
people likewise vse to eate. (Rountree, 44–45)

Similar to the Pueblo women of the Southwest, the privileged
Powhatan women wore "mantells, made both of Turkey feathers and
other fowle" (Rountree, 102). Men and women alike wore elaborate
earrings, headdresses and other ornaments that included "Fowles leggs,
Eagles, Hawks, Turkeys, etc." (79). Like the rulers in Mexico, the
Powhatan royalty included turkeys in their meals. A visitor to the
Powhatan royal palace in May 1614 reported, "That night for supper,
Powhatan's household had three does, a buck, and two cock turkeys,
which were entirely eaten up." The next morning this visitor was sent
away with "the uneaten remnants of that morning's breakfast of boiled
turkey, another whole turkey, and three baskets of bread" (109).

Like Montezuma, Powhatan collected tribute from the people he
ruled. According to John Smith, the tribute included "skinnes, beades,
copper, pearle, deare, turkies, wild beasts, and corne" (Rountree, 109).
Powhatan culture was a hierarchy, and Powhatan rulers were treated
differently from those they ruled, in death as in life. While ordinary
people were buried in the ground, individually or in groups, the ruler's
body was laid in a temple, after being disemboweled and placed on a
scaffold to decompose along with "tobacco and pipes, turkey and deer
and other victualls and pocoon" (113).

The European Assault
While it is fair to say that turkeys were not treated particularly well by
Native Americans, a worse fate awaited them under the European
invaders and their descendants, who conducted a full-scale assault
upon the species (Schorger, 54–55). Contemporary accounts tell a
story of deeds done not just for "survival" but for the sheer pleasure of
committing mayhem whenever Man met Turkey. The colonial traveler
John Josselyn wrote in the 17th century that turkeys, which had for-

merly flourished in flocks of "threescore" in Maine, were all but destroyed within twenty-five years there (Josselyn, xxx). In 1645, a New England observer reported seeing sixty broods of young wild turkeys (which would have been several hundred birds) "on the side of a Marsh, sunning of themselves in a morning betimes" (Bakeless, 242). This sight soon vanished.

John Bakeless's book, *America As Seen By Its First Explorers*, offers a vision of the world in which turkeys lived "Up the Missouri" in pre-settlement days:

> Turkeys were very tame along tributary streams like the Osage, where there were "beautiful forests full of stags and wild turkeys." The birds merely looked down from the treetops at canoes, passing down the stream near "cliffs rising high above it, with pine trees and red cedars growing in the cracks. The bald eagles soared above their tops; at the foot of these abrupt shores, pink and white mallows were reflected in the smooth mirror of the Osage River, beautifully shaded by wild vines." (366)

The beauty of these scenes, witnessed by "the eyes of discovery," did not save the turkeys, however, any more than it saved the Carolina parroquets who lived in the same region, whose green feathers gleamed on the white sycamores in the winter sunlight "like so many candles" (365), but who were fired at all the same and destroyed along with the great auk, the heath hen, the passenger pigeon, and the ivory-billed woodpecker (Bakeless, 408).

Across the continent turkeys were hunted unsparingly and sold cheap. A pound of lead shot, a bag of salt, or a bunch of pins and needles, and you got your bird (Schorger, 374–75). Town dwellers in the 17th century paid a shilling for one (Root and Rochemont, 70). In the early 19th century, the "noble bird" cost from six cents to a quarter

(Drimmer, 991; Schorger, 373–376). It took time to destroy wild turkeys to the point where their dwindling numbers began to attract notice and concern. As late as 1820, there were still so many to shoot or capture as to invite disdain. According to a source, "They were a drug on the market; in Kentucky, farm chickens cost more" (Root and Rochemont, 70).

Turkeys were eaten in all kinds of ways—stewed in raccoon fat, substituted for bread, boiled with oysters, fried in buffalo fat, and roasted with incisions filled with bear meat. Men bragged that they killed eight or ten birds with one shotgun shot, and ate only their breasts cooked in buffalo fat. One man wrote, "When we camped on a creek where wild turkeys were plentiful, we would kill fifteen or twenty and stew a potful of gizzards, hearts and livers. This was best of all, a dish fit for a king" (Schorger, 371).

As army troops, hunters, settlers, cowboys, and assorted travelers pushed through the country,[1] hunting turkeys indiscriminately and tearing down the forests in which these birds had lived for thousands of years, turkeys vanished altogether or retreated to isolated and impenetrable areas of the southeastern United States, such as the bottomland swamps of Alabama and anywhere else they could hide (Borenstein). Roosts that had once been "black" with a thousand to three thousand turkeys settled in the trees for the night, in an area a quarter of a mile wide and a mile long, became black holes as men took "all they wanted" (Schorger, 54). Turkeys disappeared under the relentless pressure from market and sport hunters who killed and crippled vast numbers of the birds and left untold numbers to rot as they went. A Texas observer wrote in 1890, "Many of them [hunters] are hunting to supply the markets, and will load a wagon at the turkey roosts in a night or two. The continued warm weather spoiled load after load before reaching the markets, the railroad being eighty-five miles distant. It is not uncommon to see the game abandoned in camp because spoiled." Often these hunters would eat some of the turkeys they killed, but soon, as a member of a party traveling through Oklahoma wrote in 1832, "they despised such small game & I have seen dead turkeys left behind on marching" (404).

In 1832, after turkeys had been already been eliminated from many of their former ranges, it was still noted that "[i]n some places, they are so numerous, as to be easily killed, beyond the wants of the people" (Wright, 357). A certain James Stuart complained in 1833, not that "the wild turkeys are shot indiscriminately" in Alabama, but that all this shooting put birds on the table that were not yet big and fat enough to enjoy dining on (Wright, 358). By 1813, Connecticut had no wild turkeys; by 1842, Vermont followed suit, along with other states. By 1920, the wild turkey had been eliminated from eighteen of the original thirty-nine states of its range, and from Ontario, Canada (Dickson, 11).

Those who routinely left records of their encounters with the bird were men. Men wrote about the excitement they felt during a turkey hunt or upon seeing a single turkey or a flock of turkeys cross into "their" domain. Though the observation was often keen, the situation was romanticized and sentimentalized, as in the following letter written by Elliott Roosevelt to his brother Theodore Roosevelt in 1875. Accompanied by eleven greyhounds, he writes, we

> struck off six or eight miles into the plains, then spreading into line we alternated dogs and horses, and keeping a general direction, beat up the small oak clumps, grass clusters, or mesquite jungles as we went along. Soon, with a loud whirr of wings, three or four turkeys rose out of the grass ahead, started up by one of the greyhounds; the rest of the party closed in from all sides; dogs and men choosing each the bird they marked as theirs. The turkey, after towering a bit, with

wings set struck off at a pace like a bullet, and with eyes fixed upwards the hounds coursed after them.

It was whip and spur for a mile as hard as horse, man, and hound could make the pace. The turkey at last came down nearer and nearer the ground, its small wings refusing to bear the weight of the heavy body. Finally, down he came and began running; then the hounds closed in on him and forced him up again as is always the case. The second flight was not a strong one, and soon he was skimming ten or even a less number of feet from the ground. Now, came the sport of it all; the hounds were bunched and running like a pack behind him. Suddenly old 'Grimbeard,' in the heart of the pack, thought it was time for the supreme effort; with a rush he went to the front, and as a mighty spring carried him up in the air, he snapped his clean, cruel fangs, under the brave old gobbler, who by a great effort rose just out of reach. One after another in the next twenty-five yards each hound made his trial and failed. At last the old hound again made his rush, sprang up a wonderful height into the air, and cut the bird down as with a knife. (Quoted in Schorger, 388)

This Victorian-style melodrama continues to color, if it no longer dominates, America's relationship with the wild turkey, which today is constituted by the scientific management approach. Wildlife biologists, conservationists, and sportsman like to boast about how they rescued the wild turkey from extinction (Sterba, A6). Virtually exterminated by the 1920s, the turkey was not only restored, "but to a record high population that is growing with no end in sight," making the bird's comeback "one of the biggest environmental success stories of the century" (Borenstein).[2]

A Civil War-era photograph in *The Wild Turkey: Biology &*
Management (Dickson, 11), published by the National Wild Turkey
Federation, tells much of the story of what happened to the wild turkey
in America. It depicts rows of dead turkeys strung upside down like
clothes on a clothesline at an army campsite. This was the fate of the
birds over and over under the assaults of the military camps. Men
slaughtered cartloads full of turkeys, shooting the birds at roost when
they were resting, sleeping and defenseless. Fifty to five hundred birds
per hunting party in a single night were boasted, with an uncounted
number of cripples left to die in the aftermath. Someone joked that
whenever the people of Colorado City wanted wild turkeys, "they
hitched a team to a wagon, drove to some stream where there was tim-
ber, ran the wagon under a turkey roost, and fired," leaving behind all
of the birds that fell beside the wagon (Schorger, 58).

A soldier in General Sheridan's post-Civil War army captured the
spirit of the times. He describes his troop's invasion of a turkey flock's
roosting grounds on the Washita River in Oklahoma as if it were a gleeful skirmish with enemy soldiers or a sportive attack on an Indian village. On the evening of December 15, 1868, he writes,

> upon the column going into camp in a heavy timber on
> the river, it was discovered that we were in the midst of
> a favorite roost of immense numbers of wild turkeys.
> The traces were everywhere visible, and some lively
> sport was anticipated when the droves returned from
> their rambles after food. Towards sunset, about fifty
> fine birds, headed, as usual, by a noble cock, appeared
> on the bluff overlooking the camp. With an air of sur-
> prise at the intrusion, the flock gathered in full view,
> apparently holding an inspection, and resolving what
> to do. At this moment, another immense flock came
> floating down from another direction, and lit in the

trees within the lines of the camp. In an instant about fifty shots were fired, killing several.

As the daylight drew nearer to a close, the turkeys, having failed to look out for other accommodations, were bent upon taking possession of their customary haunts. The numbers also increased. It was now impossible to cast the eye any where along the heavens without getting a glimpse of turkeys sailing about in the air. One drove entered the camp, running among the tents and wagons. It was decidedly amusing to witness the scene which ensued. Soldiers, teamsters, and dogs joined in the pursuit. One moment dashing under a wagon, and the next amongst the horses and mules. In the early part of the race, the turkeys had the best [of it], but, bewildered and headed off, soon became exhausted. A number were caught in this way.

While this exciting chase was going on, a party of soldiers occupied themselves with shooting at the birds as they settled in the trees, or as they approached the ground. During this fusillade, one of the volunteers, tying his horse to the picket, was somewhat astounded to find the animal jerk away from him and instantly fall to the earth. Considering all the firing and confusion, it was a matter of great surprise that no other casualties occurred. (Schorger, 161–62)

What the naturalist John Muir wrote of the passenger pigeon in the 19th century was no less true of the turkey: "Every shotgun was aimed at them" (Teale, 46). The idea conveyed in Schorger, in anecdote after anecdote, is that, whatever the circumstances, when a man saw a turkey or a flock of turkeys, he got his gun. Even if he found the turkeys somehow engaging, the man still killed them all if he could, or took a few potshots at the flock. Foreign visitors brought their guns, too. They had their muskets ready "to shoot the wild geese and turkeys" and were "always on the watch for an opportunity of practicing (on shipboard), believing that they should have such excellent sport in America shooting wild turkies" (Wright, 335).

Whole American communities gunned down turkeys and prairie chickens for eating the grain. In Ohio, people used clubs to drive turkeys from the wheat fields (Schorger, 218). Circular hunts were organized to exterminate "these famous birds of the forest" because they ate the corn. A person who grew up in Illinois wrote in 1937, "One of my earliest and most vivid recollections was of the day when everybody combined to slaughter the last immense flock of Wild Turkeys. They enticed so many tame Turkeys away and were so destructive to the crops, that their extermination was decreed by the grange, churches, and the general public" (219).

---

1. "Some cowboys in Texas attempted to keep a turkey afoot as long as possible in order to tire it out. If the bird flew, the speed of the horse was increased....Some cowboys fastened a bullet to the end of a whip and wrapped it about the turkey's neck, while others used a lasso" (Schorger, 387).

2. By 1973, when the [National Wild Turkey Federation] was founded as a tax-exempt group to promote turkey hunting, the states had built the wild-bird population up to an estimated 1.3 million birds. Conservationists called it one of the greatest species comebacks of the 20th century. And it was just the beginning. By 1990, the population was up to 3.5 million. Last year [2000] it was put at 5.4 million" (Sterba, A6).

4 ~

OUR TOKEN OF FESTIVE JOY

Thus, we see how essential the wild turkey was to the explorer, how prominent a part of the larder it proved for the early pioneers and Indians, what sport it furnished our natives, settlers and foreign sportsmen, and how early it was singled out as our token of festival joy. —Albert Hazen Wright, 336

The turkeys that graced the first Thanksgiving board in 1621 were destined to elevate the bird as the great symbol of American gratitude for the blessings of a plentiful harvest.—*Turkey Producer*, October 1960, 19

Contrary to popular belief, Thanksgiving did not become a national tradition under the Massachusetts Pilgrims; nor was the turkey for a fact the piece de resistance at the famous 1621 meal.—James G. Dickson, 10

Festive turkey? Who dreamed up that oxymoron?
—Jonathan Yardley, "Gobble Squabble."

F OLLOWING A RELATIVELY MILD SUMMER AFTER THE first terrible winter during which half the company died, the Pilgrims, who arrived at what is now Cape Cod in November of

1620, gathered their first small harvest and celebrated—though in his history of Plymouth Plantation, Governor William Bradford does not mention the Thanksgiving they held in the fall of 1621, and the actual date of it is unknown. He refers to the turkey only in passing, noting that at that time of year, "besides waterfowl there was great store of wild turkeys, of which they took many, besides venison, etc." (100).

On December 11, 1621, *Mayflower* passenger Edward Winslow wrote to a friend in England his account of the first Thanksgiving:

> Our harvest being gotten in, our Governor sent four men on fowling, that so we might after a more special manner rejoice together, after we had gathered the fruit of our labours. They four in one day killed as much fowl as, with a little held beside, served the Company almost a week. At which time, amongst other recreations, we exercised our arms, many of the Indians coming amongst us, and amongst the rest their greatest kind, Massasoit with some 90 men, whom for three days we entertained and feasted. And they went out and killed five deer which they brought to the plantation and bestowed on our Governor and upon the Captain [Myles Standish] and others" (From *Mourt's Relation*, 1622, quoted in a footnote in Bradford, 100).

Thus, while the table was full of birds that must have included turkeys, there is no specific record, as George Willison says in *Saints and Strangers*, "of the long-legged 'Turkies' whose speed of foot in the woods constantly amazed the Pilgrims" (189).

The Pilgrims did not launch Thanksgiving in America. Historian Elizabeth Pleck shrewdly documents the evolution of the holiday to the end of the 20th century in *Celebrating the Family* (21–42). For more than three centuries, Thanksgiving was a sporadic affair proclaimed off and on by various governors and churches for a variety of special occasions ranging from good health and general prosperity to victories over the Indians and the British. In the early 19th century there was still "little mention of an American Christmas and only casual notice of Thanksgiving...probably because the observance of it had not yet spread beyond the limits of New England" (Mesick, 85). Not until 1863 did President Abraham Lincoln, embroiled in the Civil War and anxious to promote national unity, proclaim Thanksgiving a national holiday. Before that, George Washington issued the first presidential Thanksgiving proclamation on October 3, 1789, John Adams issued a proclamation setting aside May 9, 1798 as a time for "fervent thanksgiving," and James Madison proclaimed January 12, 1815 as a day of prayer that the War of 1812 might end soon and peace be restored (Peterson; Love, 239–248).

A decade earlier, Alexander Hamilton, the first secretary of the Treasury, declared that "[n]o citizen of the United States should refrain from turkey on Thanksgiving Day" (quoted in Schorger, 369). Still, the turkey did not become a Thanksgiving main dish outside New England until after 1800 (368–370), any more than did Thanksgiving itself, which as late as 1900 "often passed unobserved" in many parts of the country (Pleck, 26). Even in New England the turkey was not singled out immediately as the official holiday bird. A diary account of a Thanksgiving dinner in New England in 1779 mentions in the following order, "a fine red Deer," "huge Chines of Roast Port," "a big Roast Turkey, "a Goose, & two big Pigeon Pasties" (Smith, 1966, 294). President Andrew Jackson's November 29, 1835 Thanksgiving proclamation is as teasing as Governor Bradford's in linking the turkey to the holiday. He thanked God for "the bountiful supply of wildlife with which Thou has blessed our land; for the turkeys that gobble in our forests" (quoted in Schorger, 369).

However, by 1857, the turkey had become a traditional part of the Thanksgiving holiday in New England. In that year, the English author of *Life and Liberty in America* proclaimed the bird to be, on November 22nd, "the great event of the day. As roast beef and plum pudding are upon Christmas-day in Old England, so is turkey upon Thanksgiving-day among the descendants of the Puritans in New England" (Mackay, 65).

Long before it became the Thanksgiving Day bird in America, the turkey appeared on Christmas tables in England. As early as 1573, the turkey was referred to by a contemporary as "Christmas husbandlie fare" (Wright, 338). First shipped to Europe from Mexico by the Spanish invaders in the early 16th century, the turkey was bred in Renaissance England, raised on country estates, shot in royal hunting parks for sport, and served on platters at various royal and ecclesiastical functions. The transplanted bird was then brought back to America, where it became the forerunner of modern domesticated turkeys. As Feltwell summarizes in *Turkey Farming*, "The sixteenth century saw the rapid development of turkeys, and by the seventeenth century they were common through-out the country [England] and were rapidly becoming the traditional Christmas dish" (17; also see Schorger, 467–470).

The turkey quickly entered the slaughter markets and households of England. Feasting in England meant meat, including a huge amount of bird meat and eggs. In the 17th century, every English household kept poultry, from "crammed capons" (force-fed castrated male chickens) to "little chickens."[1] Swans were "favourite ceremonial dishes, so that notable institutions in London frequently bred their own, marking them on the beak by 'necks,' or nicks." Geese were "plentiful and cheap, also turkeys" (Hartley and Elliot, 26).

For centuries, poultry were kept in London "from cellar to garret" (Jones, 1965, 82), a practice that continued into the 19th century, when "fowls were still being reared in town bedrooms" (Thomas, 95). From the 15th century on, the City of London sought to confine the poultry business to certain areas of the city due to the "grete stenche and so evel savour that it causeth grete and parlous infectying of the people and long hath done" (Jones 1965, 82). Regulations issued in 1513 forbade the poulterers of Southwark to permit their "hens, ducks, turkeycocks, or any other kind of poultry to go into the streets to 'rayse upp the myre and mucke to the common anoyauance' " (Jones 1965, 82).

The turkey's appearance in Elizabethan England's slaughter markets can be determined by looking at contemporary poultry trade association records. The London Poulters Guild, established in the 14th century, kept price control records of its live-bird inventory, showing, for instance, that on July 12, 1521, a century before the Pilgrims sailed for America, the following birds were for sale in London slaughter markets: swans, cranes, bustards, herons, bitterns, pheasants, curlews, mallards, teals, plovers, pigeons, larks, chickens, geese, snipes, and partridges (Jones 1965, 135). Turkeys weren't listed in 1521, but by 1557 the guild's records included "Turkey Chickens cocks," and in January 1571/2, "Turkey, cock[,] hen." In 1559, turkeys were added to the guild's newly regulated list of "poultry wares" (116).

In addition, the guild noted when it began giving a turkey to one of its officers as a Christmas gratuity: during the tenure of one Edward Pitts as company clerk, between 1685 and 1691, "it became customary to give the Clerk a turkey at Christmas, a present which at that time cost the Company 6s [shillings]." Around 1760, the guild reported giving its clerk seven shillings "in lieu of a turkey" on the company holiday, March 10th (Jones 1965, 50).

The turkey appears as an English household meat in Gervase Markham's handbook, *The English Housewife*, published in 1615. Chapter Two, "Of Cookery," tells the "complete housewife" all she needs to know about the "banqueting stuff, and ordering of great feasts"—everything from instructions on how to roast a fillet of veal to how to roast a cow's udder to the roasting of "a chine of beef, loin of mutton, lark, and capon at one fire, and at one instant" (87).

Markham groups turkeys together with chickens, pigeons, partridges, rails, young peahens, and "such like" as "lesser land fowl"

(123). Sauce recipes are given for turkey and for "a roast capon or turkey." Turkey is listed as a cold baked meat along with "pheasant, partridges, goose, woodcock, and such like" (122), and as a pie filling, along with "capon, pheasant, partridge, veal, peacocks, lamb, and all sorts of water fowl" (96). At "a more humble feast," as opposed to a major banquet, a roasted turkey is dish number ten following a roasted swan. Number eleven is a haunch of roasted venison, number twelve is a pastry of venison, number thirteen "a kid with a pudding in the belly," number fourteen an olive pie (made of slices of veal or other meat rolled up). Number fifteen is "a couple of capons" and number sixteen "a custard or doucets" along with other dishes and side dishes (123–124).

In the chapter "Of Cookery," Markham describes the "ordering of meats to be roasted":

> The roasting of all sorts of meats differeth nothing but in the fires, speed, and leisure...but for the ordering, preparing, and trussing your meats for the spit or table, in that there is much difference; for in all joints of meat except a shoulder of mutton, you shall crush and break the bones well; from pigs and rabbits you shall cut off the feet before you spit them, and the heads when you serve them to table, and the pig you shall chine, and divide into two parts; capons, pheasants, chickens, and turkeys you shall roast with the pinions folded up, and the legs extended; hens, stock-doves, and house-doves, you shall roast with the pinions folded up, and the legs cut off by the knees, and thrust into the bodies; quails, partridges, and all sorts of small birds shall have their pinions cut away, and the legs extended; all sorts of waterfowl shall have their pinions cut away, and their legs turned backward; woodcocks, snipes, and stints

shall be roasted with their heads and necks on, and their legs thrust into their bodies, and shovellers and bitterns shall have no necks but their heads only. (88)

In his book *Animal Revolution*, Richard Ryder offers a glimpse of how animals were prepared for meals in the typical 18th-century household establishment during the Age of Enlightenment:

[Alexander] Pope described 'kitchens covered with blood and filled with the cries of creatures expiring in tortures'. The whipping to death of pigs, in the mistaken belief that this improved the meat, was to continue in England until the following century. Turkeys were very slowly bled to death suspended upside down from the kitchen ceiling. Salmon were crimped (cut into collops while still alive), living eels skinned, and the orifices of chickens were sewn up, supposedly to fatten them. Geese repeatedly were plucked of their feathers while alive in order to provide writing quills, and many were nailed to boards for their entire lives, some with their eyes put out, while they were subjected to forced-feeding.

    Meat was cheap in England at this time and its consumption continued to be gargantuan. Receipts for large houses indicate that it was ordered by the stone [a unit of weight equal to 14 pounds] rather than the pound, and include details of the typical contemporary menu—lambs' tails for the first course for example, tongues and udders for the second, followed by ox palates with cheesecake for the third." (67)

Along with knowing how to prepare and arrange meats, Markham's housewife was required to know the "complexions of meats" (83). Those that must be "pale and white roasted" as opposed to brown roasted were "mutton, veal, lamb, kid, capon, pullet, pheasant, partridge, quail, and all sorts of middle and small land or water fowl, and all small birds" (83–84). As a "middle" or "lesser" land fowl, the turkey was a white meat bird. To obtain the "white complexion," animals were bled for hours and days. In *Man and the Natural World*, Keith Thomas writes that while cattle were normally pole-axed before slaughter, "pigs, calves, sheep and poultry died more slowly. In order to make their meat white, calves, and sometimes lambs, were stuck in the neck so that the blood would run out; then the wound was stopped and the animal allowed to linger on for another day" (93).

To become white flesh, animals were often suspended head down from the kitchen ceiling. This is how calves became veal prior to the adoption of the veal crate in the 20th century, although the fattening and softening of the flesh of lambs, piglets, birds and other farmed animals by tightly confining them in little dark sheds is an ancient practice. So-called factory farming is "new" mainly as to the number of animals used, the scale of production, and the use of antibiotics to control diseases and death rates and to bolster traditional methods of confinement, overfeeding, and selective breeding employed to force young animals to grow many times faster than normal.[2]

As Andrew Johnson points out in *Factory Farming*, the modern battery-hen building, an epitome of 20th-century animal confinement systems, is "little more than a many thousand times larger replica of the [16th-century] housewife's kitchen hen-coop which might at that date have filled in the unused space under the dresser"—"dresser" meaning the table on which meat and other foods were prepared (23).

Just as the upper classes disdained the sight and stench of the poultry stalls that littered the streets of London, so they turned a semi-blind eye to practices in their own houses. In *The Rural Life of England*,

William Howitt describes how a "delicate" 19th-century lady of his acquaintance dealt with the turkeys hanging upside down in her kitchen:

> [O]n passing the kitchen door at ten in the morning, [I] saw a turkey suspended by its heels, and bleeding from its bill, drop by drop. Supposing it was just in its last struggles from a recent death-wound, I passed on, and found the lady lying on her sofa overwhelmed in tears over a most touching story. I was charmed by her sensibility; and the very delightful conversation which I held with her, only heightened my opinion of the goodness of her heart. On accidentally passing by the same kitchen door in the afternoon, six hours afterwards, I beheld, to my astonishment, the same turkey suspended from the same nail, still bleeding, drop by drop, and still giving an occasional flutter with its wings! Hastening to the kitchen, I inquired of the cook, if she knew that the turkey was not dead. "O yes, sir," she replied, "it won't be dead, may-happen, these two hours. We always kill turkeys that way, it so improves their colour; they have a vein opened under the tongue, and only bleed a drop at a time!" And does your mistress know of this your mode of killing turkeys?" "O yes, bless you sir, it's our regular way; missis often sees 'em as she goes to the gardens—and she says sometimes, "Poor things! I don't like to see 'em, Betty; I wish you would hang them where I should not see 'em!" (45–46)

This in effect is how Charles Dickens handles the meat situation in his classic story, *A Christmas Carol,* in which the miserly Scrooge, under the aspect of the Ghost of Christmas Present, mounts a pile of flesh in a foretaste of his imminent social redemption and return to life's pleasures: "Heaped up on the floor, to form a kind of throne, were turkeys, geese, game, poultry, brawn, great joints of meat, sucking-pigs, [and] long wreaths of sausages" (303). Scrooge's first charitable act of redemption following his nightmares is to purchase "the prize Turkey" "hanging up" at the poulterer's: " 'It's hanging there now,' replied the boy. 'Is it?' said Scrooge. 'Go and buy it' " (349–350).

"Many have been the tales of the great cattle drives. Hardly anyone remembers the great turkey walks" (Karr 1998, 1999).
Before World War Two, thousands of turkeys were forced to walk to their own hanging—"two hundred turkey feet / running across to Illinois / on their way to the platter" (Mackey, ix). In Europe and America, turkeys not butchered on the farm or shot in the wild or on an estate were driven to market or to the nearest terminal on foot. In Europe as early as 1691, Cardinal Perron saw "people driving them from Languedoc [in France] to Spain in flocks like sheep" (Schorger, 466). In 18th-century Europe, turkeys were typically walked one hundred miles or more, like geese and sheep. The northern counties of England drove thousands of turkeys to the London markets on foot each fall. Margaret Visser tells how

> [f]rom the large breeding farms in Norfolk [in the northeast of England], thousands of birds crowded down the narrow roads to London during the weeks preceding Christmas. The great black Norfolk gobblers (which the English called "bubbly-jocks") wore shoes for the journey. Their feet were dipped in thick pitch or tied up in sacking and covered with little boots to protect them on the long noisy march south. (1992b)

In America prior to truck transport, turkeys were driven eight to ten miles a day through terrain ranging from densely wooded mountain trails to treeless Texas plains on journeys of fifty to two hundred or more miles (Schramm). Thousands of turkeys raised on farms in the northeast were walked fifty miles or so to Boston and nearby towns (Karr, 1997). In Tennessee and Kentucky, where these drives continued into the 1920s (Schramm), thousands of wild turkeys were captured in the hills and marched to the nearest railway station in South Carolina (Schorger, 481). Plantation owners in South Carolina drove turkeys on foot into Georgia, and in Texas, "30 men could drive a flock of 8,000 turkeys thirteen miles to market in two days" (Christman and Hawes, 17). As late as 1930, turkey flocks in Texas, Colorado, and North and South Dakota were still being herded like cattle on the prairies (Jull, 370). In Texas, the birds were gathered into flocks of approximately 20,000 and driven to distant buying stations (Schramm). The March 1930 issue of the *National Geographic Magazine* has a U.S. Department of Agriculture photograph of these so-called turkey trots, noting that

> [i]n areas where the turkey population is large, dealers send buyers into the country to gather up a drove of several hundred birds. They stop at farms, weigh the birds the farmers want to sell, add them to the drove, and drive them like cattle to the dressing plants. This practice is being discontinued, however, as the turkeys lose too much weight on long drives. (Jull, 348)

How were all these turkeys kept together during these long, arduous journeys? In addition to being hardy and able to negotiate difficult terrain, including swimming if need be (Schorger, 178–179), turkeys are flock birds who walk more than they fly in their daily excursions. As well as being able to fly fifty miles an hour, turkeys can easily run twelve miles an hour (Madson, 57–58). Reports show wild turkeys walking together towards their nightly roosting places, crossing fields and even running up the sides of mountains in troops ranging from twenty to 200 to a thousand birds (Schorger, 186–187). Turkeys have been described wading across streams in single file and flying over lakes and rivers, up to a mile wide, to get where they were going (178–179). Like the passenger pigeons in the sky before they were exterminated, wild turkeys in Oklahoma and Texas, where they were most abundant, "covered the prairies for miles" (55). The bird's amiability, vigorous constitution, and long, strong legs made these drives possible.

Ideally a drive of 20,000 turkeys employed four to six drovers, two for every thousand birds, forty drovers in all "calling out gee and haw and git / to them as if they / were mules" (Mackey, ix). The drovers carried long whips with strips of flannel tied to the ends, which they used to "flick" the birds in line (Schramm). Often a red cloth was tied to the end of the whip or stick because turkeys have an aversion to red. This "red flag" was said to act on the birds "as a scourge to a quadruped" (Schorger, 155–156), aided by dogs.

Kathleen Karr's children's book *The Great Turkey Walk* describes a walk of some 500 to a thousand turkeys from Missouri to Denver in 1863. The owner (accounts differ) rounded up his birds in Iowa and Missouri, filled a horse-and-mule-drawn wagon with shelled corn, and employed two boys to drive them to Denver, 600 miles away. At night the turkeys roosted in the surrounding trees or on the wagon, while others "lay limp on the sand" as they approached the town (Schorger, 483). At dawn, the birds chased grasshoppers. It is unclear how many turkeys actually made it to Denver. In Karr's story, the pedestrian flock is besieged by everything from circus bandits to army troops to foxes and coyotes. However, as the book charts the course of a burgeoning young capitalist hewing his way to becoming a prosperous American turkey farmer, most of the turkeys not only get there, but they march to their fate in style—as if proud to be a part of this facet of American history. A point always made about these drives was that if the birds were not successfully regrouped each morning upon leaving their roosts, they scattered in the woods and fields and could not be recovered (Schorger, 481).

In addition, the birds' determination to roost every night at dusk had to be accommodated. A New Hampshire historian writes about how, at an exact point in the evening, "suddenly the whole drove with one accord rose from the road and sought a perch in the neighboring trees. The drover was prepared for such a halt and drew up his wagon beside the road, where he passed the night" (E. Gilbert [1907] quoted in Schorger, 480).

As well as being walked to markets like the Cincinnati, Ohio market described in Frances Trollope's *Domestic Manners of the Americans* (60–61), turkeys were slaughtered on farmsteads, a practice that continues today alongside industrial mass production during the holidays. Turkeys were slaughtered for home consumption and for buyers—the local community and city and town dwellers. The coming of mechanical refrigeration in the late 19th century facilitated the transportation of poultry carcasses in cold storage to distant markets and affected farm practice as well. Prior to the invention of the icebox, farmers killed, bled, and defeathered their birds in the fall, then hung them from a rafter in the summer kitchen to keep them from rotting until they were eaten, which had to be soon. A 1960 turkey trade magazine cites this former dependence on cold weather as a primary reason why turkey consumption was largely limited to Thanksgiving and Christmas ("Early Turkey Slaughter"). This was an obstacle to an industry seeking to put "more turkey in every stomach every day of every week of every month during the year" ("World Meat Production").

Before they were killed, the birds were, as they still are, starved for approximately twelve hours in order to empty their digestive tracts to reduce the splatter of the gastrointestinal contents during killing (Mercia, 84). While many farmers simply chopped the bird's head off with an axe on a tree stump, as depicted in a photograph in the March

1930 issue of *National Geographic Magazine* (Jull, 347), "older methods of cutting off the head or wringing the neck" were used alongside
the customary and commercial practice of suspending turkeys and
other farm fowl head down by their feet from a shackle and killing
them that way, a method comprising "first, that of cutting or bleeding;
and second, that of sticking or braining, which paralyzes the...chickens,
fowl, ducks, geese and turkeys" (Benjamin and Pierce, 139).

*Farm Poultry: A Popular Sketch of Domestic Fowls for the Farmer and
Amateur,* published in 1901, explains to the home slaughterer, or
"dresser," how to prepare birds with the least amount of blood, as
"Americans prefer to have all flesh free from blood" (Watson, 286),
although in reality a considerable amount of blood remains in the cap-
illaries of flesh after death (Heath). First, it was necessary to suspend
the birds in such a way that they would not strike against each other or
other hard object with their wings while flopping and flapping, which
could cause bruising and broken bones as well as interfering with
killing. A common method of restraining and bleeding the birds (a
method that is still recommended for small farm operations) was to
suspend the bird in a metal funnel, or "killing cone," with the head
protruding at the bottom, weighed down by a four-pound blood cup
hooked to the bird's lower beak (Mercia, 86). The purpose of the blood
cup is "to prevent the bird from bending its neck and swallowing blood
during the involuntary convulsions subsequent to slaughter"
(Benjamin and Pierce, 141).

In braining, the beak was pried open and a cut was made through
the roof of the mouth through a carotid artery or jugular vein to the
base (rear lobe) of the brain with a knife. The knife was then twisted in
the brain in order to paralyze rather than to anesthetize or kill the bird
in order to facilitate immobilization and feather release: "It is necessary
that the brain be pierced with a knife so that the muscles of the feather follicles are paralyzed, allowing the feathers to come out easily." This
paralysis-inducing procedure is now done with electricity following the

development of the method in the 1930s (Benjamin and Pierce, 139). In either case the birds were, as they still are, kept alive through the slaughtering process and tortured to death in a state of paralysis or partial paralysis (Skewes and Birrenkott; Davis *Prisoned Chickens*, 115–121). Slow death is integral to animal farming practice in any case. As Arabella the pig farmer's daughter tells Jude in the pig-killing episode in Thomas Hardy's novel *Jude the Obscure*, "The meat must be well bled, and to do that he must die slow" (86–87).

Dry-picking was the most common method of removing the feathers. Its purpose was to retain the thin epidermal layer of the skin that the other method of loosening feathers, scalding, destroys, resulting in a dry "unsightly" carcass (Small, 467).

After sticking and braining, which was also done by inserting a knife through the bird's lower eyelid to the brain (Benjamin and Pierce, 141),[3] the slaughterer began "picking"—pulling the feathers out of the live bird, sometimes preceded by a blow to the bird's head (Watson, 286).

A problem in preparing turkeys and chickens before the advent of white birds and automated singes was the dark pigment of the skin and the tiny pin feathers (Weiss, H1, H7), which were considered unattractive, causing "[m]any experienced housewives...to spend considerable time in 'pinning' the bird and getting it ready for roasting" (Small, 467).

Birds slaughtered but not eaten at the farm were delivered directly to customers or transported by rail to "commission men," who sold them to city retailers (Watson, 292). In many places, just before Thanksgiving, a "turkey day" was held. The day before, farmers killed and dressed their turkeys (that is, they plucked and bled the birds while retaining the head, feet, and internal organs), then took them to town the next morning to be bid on. As new processing techniques were developed and automobiles came into use in the 1930s, live turkeys were packed in crates at the farm and trucked to central slaughtering facilities. By 1930, turkeys and other poultry were being shipped by rail in 2,800 specially designed cars; by 1956, these cars had been replaced by trucks (Skinner, 708). A turn-of-the-century manual suggested that birds shipped to market by rail should be placed in coops "high enough to permit the fowls to stand erect...and give comfort to the occupants of the coop" (Watson, 297). Today, the nine billion birds being shipped to slaughter each year in the United States receive no such consideration of their comfort.[4]

As we turn from these scenes to the Thanksgiving Day table and its occupants, the trail gets wiped pretty clean. It would take a metaphysical version of a modern blood detector to trace the path leading to the roasted turkey being placed on the table by the ideal grandmother before the ideal American family, the grandfather standing helpfully behind, and towering gently over, his wife, his children, his grandchildren, his table, and his turkey, with his carving knife just below view. This is the famous scene depicted in Norman Rockwell's November 27, 1943 painting featured on the cover of the *Saturday Evening Post* (See Pleck, 35–36).

Hard as it may be for many of us to recall now, the carver until fairly recently was a figure of crucial stylistic importance to festive occasions such as Thanksgiving. In *The Rituals of Dinner*, Margaret Visser writes that historically, the carver, who ceremonially divided the meat before the company, was the "focus of everyone's attention" (1992a, 234). This was because, for thousands of years, meat "was placed before the family as a result of male enterprise and triumph; and men, with their knives...insisted on carving it up, and even cooking it before the expectant and admiring crowd" (231). Hierarchy was an integral part of the carving ceremony; hence, in the Middle Ages, the carver was of noble birth, a friend of the lord of the manor, or a relative, whose role was "theatrical and ornamental as well as practical" (234–235).

In the history of ceremony, the Thanksgiving Turkey is a type of the symbolic great bird featured at ritual feasts going back to the Middle Ages and beyond. In medieval France, a "great bird" such as a peacock, swan, heron, crane, or pheasant was sworn over by the lord and his male guests before being carved. The bird could be alive and decorated with a jeweled collar or dead when the oath was taken. At the Duke of Burgundy's Vow of the Pheasant in 1434, the "diners and co-conspirators" swore their vows over a live pheasant before killing, carving, and consuming the bird (Visser, 1992a, 234).

To cut and present a large bird or other ceremonial animal was to "do the honours" at medieval and Renaissance festive meals. Manuals gave elaborate instructions on how to carve up a creature to be fit for a prince. The carver "lifted the entire joint or fowl up into the air, speared on the carving fork held in his left hand, and sliced pieces off it by wielding an extremely sharp knife in his right; wafers of meat fell to the small plate underneath...in perfectly organized patterns" (Visser 1992a, 235–236).

Today, the art of carving is largely a lost one outside the restaurant trade, although "fathers may still be called upon to stand and divide the turkey or the joint" at Christmas or Thanksgiving (Visser 1992a, 241). By the 1940s, the carving of the turkey, though a function that was still patriarchal if no longer princely, had become problematic enough to spark jokes aimed at the carver. That the carver should be composed as well as skilled, if not elaborately so, could no longer be counted on by the paterfamilias, his family, and friends. At that point, all eyes were upon him, and a Rabelaisian chorus surrounded him. A 1947 cartoon sequence in the *New York Times* joked in "To Carve a Turkey," that "[a]ll over the land, as usual on that date [Thanksgiving day], carvers will be exposed to humiliation and contempt, bad advice and insult" (Pearson), and a 1954 *New York Times* "Fuss 'n' Feathers" quipped, "It is not alone the fact that the amateur carver misses the joints and tries to cut through the largest bones, that fills him with regret and his lap full of sage and onions. It is the horrible thought that the entire company is looking at him" (Bill Nye quoted in Rodman). (One might also add that there is no horror or regret at having body parts splattered in his lap.)

During the last quarter of the 20th century, ridicule ranked with sentimental piety in the prevailing rhetoric of the Thanksgiving Day ritual. If nobody really hates a bungling turkey carver as long as the food gets served, the drama played out between the carver, the carved, and the dining chorus is a ritual of dinner that could be said to reveal, as well as to conceal, the "determination of each person present to be a diner, not a dish" (Visser 1992a, 4).

Beneath such determination lurks perhaps the primal anxiety that one could so easily be transformed from a happy "gobbler" to the hapless "gobbled," from the presiding Sage to the victim stuffed with sage, an object of both sarcasm and sacrifice, a reminder that the knife cuts both ways. The irony in the connection is that both carver and turkey are vulnerable somebodies with whom others can readily identify and insensate somethings with which one does not identify. The bungling turkey carver symbolizes in a trivial but not meaningless caricature a synthesis of these two aspects.

The turkey is not America's official national bird; the bald eagle of North America was adopted by Congress in 1782. However, the turkey has become an American symbol, rivaling the bald eagle in actual, if not formal, significance. The bird is ceremonially linked to Thanksgiving, the oldest holiday in the United States. Yet, unlike the bald eagle, the turkey is not a symbol of prestige or power. Nor, despite frequent claims, is there any evidence that Benjamin Franklin seriously promoted the turkey as the national bird—more "respectable" than the bald eagle, whatever he may have felt—except as a passing jest in a letter to his married daughter, Sarah Bache, on January 26, 1784, two years after the bald eagle had already been adopted (Smith, 1986).

While, as we have seen, the wild turkey has a long history of involvement with Native American, Colonial American, and European cultures, today the bird is invoked primarily in order to disparage the commercially raised factory-farmed turkey. Little has changed since the consumer newsletter *Moneysworth* proclaimed on November 26, 1973:

"When Audubon painted it, it was a sleek, beautiful, though odd-headed bird, capable of flying 65 miles per hour....Today, the turkey is an obese, immobile thing, hardly able to stand, much less fly. As for respectability, the big bird is so stupid that it must be taught to eat, and so large in the breast that in order to breed, a saddle must be strapped to the hen to offer the turkey-cock a claw-hold" ("Light and Dark").[5]

Each year this litany of sarcasm accompanies the sentimentality around Thanksgiving. Each year the media pour venom on the Thanksgiving Day bird. In the 20th century, America celebrated its heritage by feasting on a bird it despised, a bird that was said to be a more honest reflection than the bald eagle of American taste and technology (Weiss, H1). If yesterday it was certain ethnic populations, foreigners, and bungling turkey carvers we insulted, today we can count on the likelihood that all over the land, as usual on Thanksgiving, turkeys will be exposed to humiliation, contempt, and insult.

Thanksgiving has other functions, but one thing it does is to formalize a desire to kill someone we hate and to make a meal out of that someone. In this role, the turkey dinner is not that far distant from a cannibal feast, that "strange mixture of honor and hatred" in which not a few cultures in the history of the world have disposed of their enemies and relatives in ceremonial fashion (Sagan, 21).

Many of the people to whom I mention this "hatred of the turkey" idea say they never noticed it before, or, if they did, they didn't give it any thought. Such obliviousness illustrates, in part, the idea that the "most successful examples of manipulation are those which exploit practices which clearly meet a felt—not necessarily a clearly understood—need among particular bodies of people" (Hobsbawm and Ranger, 307).

In the case of Thanksgiving, the need is not so much to eat turkey, which many people complain about, but to rationalize an activity that, despite every effort to make the turkey seem more like a turnip, has failed "on purpose" to obliterate the bird into just meat. To do so would diminish the bird's dual role in creating the full Thanksgiving experience. In order to affect people properly, a sacrificial animal must not only be eaten by them; the animal's death must be "witnessed by them, and not suffered out of sight as we now arrange matters." But since this is how we now arrange matters, attention must somehow be "deliberately drawn, by means of ritual and ceremony," to the reality of the animal's life and the "performance of killing" (Visser, 1992a, 32).

This is why, in order to be ritually meaningful, the bird continues to be culturally constructed as a sacred player in our drama about ourselves as a nation, at the same time that we insist that the bird is a nobody, an anonymous "production animal."[6] According to Margaret Visser, "what is meant by 'sacrifice' [is] literally the 'making sacred' of an animal consumed for dinner." No wonder that any mention of cannibalism in connection with eating turkeys or any other animals provokes a storm of protest, given that, as Visser says, cannibalism to the Western mind is "massively taboo," more damnable than incest (1992a, 5). However, cannibalism, transposed to the consumption of a nonhuman animal, is a critical, if largely unconscious, component of America's Thanksgiving ritual.

America knows somehow that it has to manage its portion of humanity's primeval desire to have "somebody" suffer and die ritualistically for the benefit of the community or nation at a time when the consumption of nonhuman animals has become morally problematic in the West as well as industrialized to the point where the eaters can barely imagine the animals involved in their meal. It is ironic, as Visser points out, that "people who calmly organize daily hecatombs of beasts, and who are among the most death-dealing carnivores the world has ever seen," are shocked by the slaughtering of animals in other cultures (1992a, 32). The following chapter looks at the role of turkey taunting at Thanksgiving in light of this irony.

1. In Thomas Hardy's novel *Tess of the d'Urbervilles,* Tess's winter farm chores include "plucking fowls, or cramming turkeys and geese." Ch. 15, 124.

2. Antibiotics pump up birds artificially by retaining water in their cells and by disturbing the composition and interactions of their intestinal microflora, thereby upsetting normal relations between bacteria and host. Davis, 1996d, 103. See also Nicols Fox, *Spoiled,* 151, 158–162.

3. "One of the best methods of locating the proper direction in which to make an eye stick is to remove a flight feather from the wing of a dead bird, insert the quill beneath the eyeball and probe gently until it passes through into the skull via the optic canal" (Benjamin and Pierce, 141).

4. 8,718,704,000 birds were slaughtered in federally inspected slaughter plants in 2000, including 8,261,114,000 young chickens ("broilers"), 165,027,000 spent commercial laying hens and breeding chickens (roosters and hens), 268,069,000 turkeys, and 24,494,000 ducks. The total number of mammals killed, including cattle, calves, pigs, and sheep, was 139.2 million animals. These slaughter figures do not include the millions of birds and mammals slaughtered in state-inspected facilities or in small farm operations, and they do not include the millions who die before reaching the slaughterhouse, including the half billion unwanted "egg-type" male chicks destroyed at birth in the hatcheries each year in the U.S. In addition, 14,307,000 pounds of "other poultry" were slaughtered, including ostriches, emus, geese, pigeons, rabbits, and other miscellaneous categories of birds. USDA/NASS.

5. In the 1930s, '40s, and '50s, canvas saddles were strapped on the backs of female breeding turkeys "to prevent damage from the male's feet as he attempted to mate. These saddles were abandoned during the 1950s [and replaced with artificial insemination] when it became clear that [because the male became too big to mate properly] natural mating was no longer producing economic levels of fertility" (Bakst and Wishart, 4). A photo of saddled turkey hens on range appears in Marsden and Martin, 165.

6. Thus the National Turkey Federation vacillates from one year to the next over whether to name or not to name the White House turkey. Which is better for business? To personalize the bird used in the presidential pardoning ceremony or to represent him as a nameless "production animal rather than a pet"? (Trueheart, B6).

5 —

WHY DO WE HATE THIS
CELEBRATED BIRD?

Unanimous hatred is the greatest medicine for a human community.—Aeschylus, *Eumenides* (quoted in Girard, 126)

[M]en can almost never share peacefully an object they all desire, but they can always share an enemy they all hate because they can join together in destroying him, and then no lingering hostilities remain, at least for a while.—René Girard, *Violent Origins*, 128

I love the bird, and I deeply resent the way it has become synonymous with failure, the butt of cruel jokes, reputed to be among the stupidest of animals.—Peter Perl 1995, *Washington Post Magazine*, 36

Anyone who's ever met a live specimen, knows the turkey fits the bill for just the kind of animal we want to eat.—Evelyn Hall, *Weekend Plus*, 4

[W]e have absolutely no problem eating them. When you get to know turkeys, they're amazingly stupid and mean.—Jane Fleck, a turkey farmer (Perry)

D ESPITE MUCH BACKSLIDING, OPPOSITION TO
abusive behavior and a broadening definition of abuse
appear to be growing in America. Injuries and injustices that
went unnoticed in the recent past, cruelties openly inflicted with
impunity and even praise, are increasingly unacceptable and, in many
cases, now illegal in our society. Child abuse, spousal abuse, abuse of
minorities and women, abuse of the environment, sexual abuse, animal
abuse—these are not just catch phrases and a lumping together of dis-
parate entities and categories. They reflect changes in the moral climate
of our culture. Not only physical abuse but the malice that constitutes
an abusive attitude is apparently deemed less tolerable. This includes
malicious humor as well as an "increasing recognition of the damage
that hate speech inflicts on its intended victims" (Comninou, 134).

People who desire to be cruel are increasingly on the defensive.
Those wishing to be snide at the expense of victims society has begun
to sympathize with—and the range of informed and intuitive sympa-
thies appears to be growing, not shrinking—must deflect hostility that
could justifiably be directed against themselves instead. One way of
doing this is to ridicule the victims' defenders. One can deride them
and their concerns without inquiry simply by calling them "politically
correct"—spoiling everyone's fun by being too "puritanical" about justice, too rigorously protective of the defenseless. In such cases, those
who are exercising conventional behavior represent themselves ironically as the liberated ones.

To the extent that one's audience shares one's view of a particular
class of victims, one need not worry about being held accountable or
about having one's facts straight, or about making any sense: "People
like elbow room," but "birds like to be in flocks" (poultry specialist
quoted in Manning, *USA Today*). If called to account not just for one's
facts but also for one's attitude, all that need be said in reply is "light-
en up" or "get a life." In situations involving nonhuman animals, where
such attitudinal liberty is still the norm, animal liberation is not human

liberation. Although this is starting to change, whenever the subject is animals (and certain classes of animals in particular), as Carol J. Adams observes in *Neither Man Nor Beast*, "people with the most ignorance still are able to set the limits of the discussion" (1995a, 111). She asks, "What exactly do corpse eaters know" about the animals they eat and dismiss (112)? Let us look at what people who "know" turkeys exploitatively have to say about them.

> A turkey is too mentally unendowed to even stand upright (Brush, F8). Turkeys are dumb. They have beady eyes, they are unpersonable, they smell bad (Hall, 4). The turkey is amazingly stupid and mean; frail, stupid, mean; the snood hangs off his beak in a thoroughly disgusting way (Perry). It's easy to train wild turkeys to stay on a treadmill; they aren't the most intelligent animals (Marchetti). Turkeys are humongous mutants (Weiss, H1), too clumsy to mate (Fritz). All turkeys do is stand around and look stupid, because they are stupid (Zucco, 3D). They know the necessity of eating and drinking, but other than that, the rest is stupidity. Turkeys are cannibals. Your basic tame turkey: a big, blocky character, slightly rumpled, heavy-breasted, short-legged, short-necked, meaty—and dumb. What other bird would stand in a heavy down-pour, look up into the rain, open its beak wide and drown on its feet? (Mizejewski)

How do turkeys feel about being forcibly subdued in order to be manually masturbated and inseminated three times a week? "They don't mind it....They find it pleasing....Some turkeys actually get so excited by the mere arrival of the milkers [i.e. masturbators] that they cannot be milked in time" (Perl, 1995, 16).[1]

Anthropology has shown that, determined to do violence to an innocent victim, societies must first turn the victim into someone who deserves such treatment, who at some mysterious level even "willed" being placed in an adversarial, self-destructive relationship with the destroyer. Be they "noble" or "dumb," animals throughout history have been acquiescing at the sacrificial altar in human narratives, inviting hunters to chase and kill them, begging people to eat them, and "contracting" with humans to domesticate them and determine their fate. And they have been despised for it, even the so-called noble ones. As Joy Williams writes in "The Inhumanity of the Animal People," "Their mysterious otherness has not saved them, nor have their beautiful songs and coats and skins and shells, nor have their strengths, their skills, their swiftness, the beauty of their flights" (1997, 60).

According to a hunter, the turkey, though inheriting wildness, retains it only by "constant external stimulation" (Schorger, 140). In fact, once we start looking at the turkey, the categories of "wild" and "tame," "wild" and "domesticated," get fuzzy. The bird the early European explorers and colonists encountered was not the bird that dominates modern hunters' discourse. In anecdote after anecdote from the 17th through the 19th centuries, the wild turkey is characterized as showing an almost Disneyesque friendliness towards people. As John Madson says in the Smithsonian, "Wild turkeys, as the first settlers found them, were as trusting and unwary as they were plentiful" (54). A record of observations bears this out.

> Wild turkeys drinking at the river were so undisturbed by a nearby hunter that he took away their broods of chicks without difficulty. They came so close to people they could be shot with a pistol. They showed indifference to fires built where they roosted. They were notoriously indifferent to disturbance at roost, which made shooting them at night very popular. They appeared to

hover near our fire so we killed them. Nelson near Durango had the experience of seeing an old male turkey continuing to walk towards his campfire though it was not killed until several shots had been fired. Wild turkeys would come to our house and roost in the trees with the chickens and domestic turkeys. They often sat with their young on my fences so trustingly that I found it difficult to bring myself to shoot them. They evinced no particular alarm, nothing like that which one of these birds would be apt to show at the present time under similar circumstances. Merriam's turkey in Mexico originally showed no more wariness than its eastern relative. Turkeys could be so trusting that an observer might believe they were domestic (Schorger, 133–136).

It isn't that these wild birds weren't alert, savvy, and fully capable of living successfully in a natural environment, collectively as populations and as individuals; they were. They just hadn't yet learned to live under a relentless human assault. Absent "constant external stimulation," the wild turkey has a tendency to revert to the trustfulness of its ancestors. By the same token, "[i]t is not uncommon for domestic turkeys to revert to the wild" (Schorger, 144). Allowed to wander, domestic turkeys "became so wary that they could be recovered only by shooting" (145).

The 20th-century disdain for the domestic turkey was held by a 19th-century hunter regarding the wild turkey, which he considered a "stupid, unwary bird" (Schorger, 134). Who could respect a fowl whose flocks maintained their repose upon the sand as steamships rolled along the Mississippi? Another hunter based his opinion of the wild turkey on what he regarded as the bird's foolish behavior in the course of being chased by men, dogs, and guns: "I think most of those who have given their attention to this bird will agree with me," he loftily declared, "that they are the wildest and the tamest, the most cunning and wary, and the most stupid and foolish of all birds. The first two or three times starting him, he will put himself in the air the moment he hears or sees you, if half a mile away. Shoot at him every time you see or hear him, and he will soon become demoralized and then find some tree-top, or place to hide, and if his head is out of sight, all right, he will permit the dog to point him, and be kicked out within fifteen or twenty steps of the hunter" (146–147). Note the contempt in this report: What a dope that turkey is. He asked for it. Foolish ploys trying to hide himself. He didn't really mean No. He "permitted" the dog....

What then is a wild turkey? In *A View to a Death in the Morning: Hunting and Nature Through History*, Matt Cartmill says that the word "wild" can mean many things, "but for the hunter's purposes, a wild animal is one that is not docile—that is, not friendly toward people or submissive to their authority. No other criterion of wildness counts in hunting. The game animals on a private hunting estate may be some-one's legal chattels, but they still count as wild beasts for the hunter so long as they run from him. Even domesticated livestock can be fair game for the hunter if they have 'run wild,' like the pigs in *Lord of the Flies*" (29).

However, the turkey defies even these shifting categories. The original wild turkeys were strong, swift, and able, but they were also, in a sense, docile. If not exactly submissive to human authority, they were, or they tried to be, friendly to people. They showed "primitive unwariness to man" (Schorger, 133). For this, however, they were nei-ther respected nor protected. On the contrary, because of their amenable character, turkeys were easily trapped and penned, and when the owners grew tired of eating them, they were often left to starve and die (403).

The modern habit of despising the turkey is therefore not new, but a variation on a theme in American folklore. Prior to the 20th-century revival of the bird Americans nearly drove to extinction, the turkey got mixed reviews as a game bird, with an accent on disparagement. Turkey hunters and the United States Department of Agriculture say that while the Southwest and Northern Indians esteemed the bird, American Indians such as the Cherokee and the Apache scorned turkey meat and despised the turkey as a cowardly, timid bird, unworthy of their prowess and status (Marsden, 54; "Turkey Trivia").

The wild turkey of today is as much a rhetorical invention as it is an aboriginal species that has been "restored." Restoration of decimated flocks has involved extensive manipulation of the bird and its habitat: supplemental winter feeding, including various special types of feeders and shelters; controlled burning of forests; planting of grain crops; well-drilling; wing-clipping; leg-bands; neck-bands; use of breeding enclosures; artificial incubation; artificial insemination; culling of captive-raised birds to conform to shifting and competing standards of "purity" and "wildness" ranging from color to cunning; transfer of pen-raised poults and wild-captured adults from one place to another using traps, nets, airplane drops, anesthetizing and immobilizing drugs; release of thousands of game-farm hybrid turkeys and "surplus gobblers" prior to hunting season (Schorger, 68, 404, 410–428, 456). Not surprisingly, the combination of direct human interventions, random matings, turkey escapes, and vanishings has resulted in "stock of doubtful purity," wildness "tainted with domestic blood" (Schorger, 417), introduction of diseases to wild turkey populations (337), and "many instances where 'domestic' genes were introduced into Eastern wild turkey populations" (Christman and Hawes, 14).

Despite the effort to recreate or to construct a "true wild turkey," distinct from, and superior to, its commercialized domestic cousins, the so-called wild bird keeps revisiting the human scene, walking around in suburbia, midtown, the Bronx. "Wild turkeys have proved to be more adaptable than we ever thought," according to a biologist.

"They often seem unperturbed by people, especially when tempted by a feast and not chased by dogs or guns" (Brodie, C6).

This interaction is to be welcomed, unless it becomes an excuse for further assaults on the bird.[2] Jonathan Yardley's "Gobble Squabble" is typical turkeyday humor: "In all likelihood it is to the stupidity of turkeys that the ghastly custom of eating them at Thanksgiving can be traced. When the Pilgrims and the Indians sat down to their celebratory repast lo these many years ago, they ate wild turkeys that had been shot for the occasion, probably because the turkeys wandered into town wearing signs that read SHOOT ME."

Let us look further back for just a minute. The mythology of antiquity offers two opposing models of the human–nonhuman animal relationship central to this discussion: the Orphic model and the Dionysian model. The Dionysian model is based on the primitive god Dionysus, the Greek personification of intoxication, ferocity, and the chase. Followers of Dionysus were famous for their frenzied dismemberment and devouring of live prey. Wild animals fled from their Dionysian pursuers, scattering in fear in all directions prior to being torn apart when caught.

The legendary Orpheus was not a god but a mortal revered for the godlike, peace-bringing power of his music. Each morning Orpheus greeted the sun with his song. His melodies attracted the birds and other wild creatures, and even the mountains were moved by his music. The poet Ovid tells how "with his singing Orpheus drew the trees, / The beasts, the stones, to follow..." (Book 11, 259).

Orpheus charmed animals, but he did not deceive them. He lured animals to himself, but not to harm them. It is easy to imagine the turkey among the animals Orpheus would have charmed, because the turkey is drawn to music, of which there are some interesting accounts—like this one by musician Jim Nollman: "I went to Mexico for a while, and lived next door to a family who kept a turkey in their yard. Every time I would hit a certain high note while practicing on my flute, the turkey would gobble. I spent a month playing music beside this turkey....Eventually I noticed he would stand by the fence, waiting for me to arrive and play" (Bartlett, 7; see also Wickersham).

Dionysus and his followers, which included the Maenads, the "Raving Women," also lured animals to themselves, as well as chasing them. These manic embodiments of "false Orpheus," who finally tore Orpheus to pieces, causing the birds and "throngs of beasts" to weep for him (Ovid, Book 11, 260), drew the denizens of the forests and fields from their hiding places to suckle and soothe them as part of a destructive seduction ritual (Detienne, 62). It is easy to imagine the turkey among the animals fooled by their wiles, as the turkey's allurability is a primary attraction of turkey hunting: "The name of the game is calling the bird close....That's the rush" (Stout).

An example of "false Orpheus" in today's world appeared in the *Wall Street Journal* a few years ago, complete with sunrise songs and a modern Maenad, a "Miss Daulton" from Kansas:

> By the time the sun was above the horizon, Mr. Keck ["Mr. Turkey"] was masterfully filling the air with the excited yelps, clucks and purrs of the loneliest of turkey hens. Each note brought responding gobbles from the assorted toms that were keeping company with a flock of hens that had flown from the trees and down onto the prairie. After a suspenseful stalemate, a pair of toms stepped into view 200 yards away. Both Mr. Keck and his hunting partner watched in amazement as the birds closed the distance, strutting with tails fanned in half-circles and their body feathers, each of which glowed iridescently in the early light, standing on end. When the two toms were so close the hunters could see the excitement in their pea-sized eyes, a well-aimed shot dropped the biggest of the birds....

When the hunter stood and removed her head net, a beautiful face framed by lush, raven hair emerged...."It's the most exciting hunting I've ever done, definitely," said Miss Daulton. (Pearce, 1995)[3]

Melodrama apart, it may be asked how shooting a creature walking straight at you constitutes "hunting," or how luring an animal under false pretenses could be considered "sporting," any more than "putting out poisoned hay for them" could be so construed (Cartmill, 29). For a turkey hunter, "the excitement and the thrill of hearing an old long-beard drum as he stalks the hen of his dreams" consists in the imminent prospect of the kill (Dickson, 415):

Her call fills Tom with feelings he can't control. By the time he calls back, he's burning with desire. She gives him a coy purr, setting off paroxysms of passion deep inside him. He throbs with lust for her. He has to have her. Now!

Tom rushes toward her, expecting the Julia Roberts of wild turkeys. Instead, it's Roy Rhodes, professional turkey caller, scratching a rosewood striker across a piece of artificial slate, a 12-gauge shotgun resting on his knee. (Sterba, A1)

Teasing "love sick" turkeys with sirens' songs is a key element of the euphoria leading to the climax of pulling the trigger in turkey hunting. Here sex is used to degrade and destroy for the sake of cruelty, pleasure, and the sensation of power. "Shall he pretend to be a tom on the make, thereby stirring another male's aggressive hormones and bringing him into the open in the mood for a fight? Or shall he use another, more tender sound, hoping to rouse feathery tumescence and cause the tom to throw caution to the woodland winds in pursuit of romance" (Stout).

Turkey hunters brag about the erotic pleasure they get from mimicking turkey courtship behavior, imitating a "hot hen" so that a lovesick tom will "offer its head and neck for a shot." They talk about killing the birds for "love": "Let it be stated now that, because of the fowl he loves, the technology of hunting has advanced by light-years. There are turkey-hunting seminars and videos, new types of camouflage, new firearms, new ways to use old firearms. And new ways to call turkeys to their doom" (Stout).

No doubt the paraphernalia of mimicry, gadgetry, and language is designed to focus less attention on the turkey than on the hunter for whom the bird is a mere object (Riordan, "Patents"). At the same time, it is necessary that the hunter experience the bird as a someone, a creature who in return experiences the hunter and the hunter's pursuit, just as in conventionally recognized hate and sex crimes, apathy and empathy combine psychologically in the perpetrator.

Taking animal victims seriously in our society is still largely taboo. For one thing, people are scared. If those guys weren't out there shooting turkeys they'd be inside beating up their wives. For many people, nonhuman animals are still regarded as acceptable substitutes for the discharging of human rage: let animals take the heat—the hit—instead of us. Such was the attitude of the child psychologist and Nazi concentration camp analyst Bruno Bettelheim, who wrote about what he considered the danger of becoming too civilized:

> As a matter of fact, the chances for discharging violent tendencies in socially approved ways at least vicariously are now so severely curtailed that their regular and safe discharge is no longer possible....Rural life used to offer the child at least a chance for some vicarious discharge of violence: in my native Austria, slaughtering the pig

was a distinct highlight in the lives of peasant children. (193–194)

Unfortunately, slaughtering pigs does not seem to have prevented many rural youths from joining the Nazis and contributing to the evil that Bettelheim sought ways to prevent in the future. It may be, contrary to Bettelheim's theory, that the pleasure of pig sticking contributed to the evil.

The involvement of sex in the hunting of turkeys, whose natural courtship and mating behavior is a far cry from the artificiality of contemporary breeding farms, shows that the wild bird is as vulnerable to human sexual violence and degradation as the domestic turkey is. Consider the following account of the manual insemination and semen collection process by which all or virtually all modern commercial turkeys are now produced.[4] The place is a ConAgra[5] breeding facility in Missouri.

> Two men herded them—a hundred or so at a time— into a makeshift pen. From there, the "drivers" forced five to six birds at a time into a chute which opened onto a concrete pit. They put me to work first in the pit, grabbing and "breaking" the hens. I had to reach into the chute, grab a hen by the legs, and hold her— ankles crossed—in one hand, as she beat her wings and struggled. Holding her on the edge of the pit, I wiped my other hand over her rear, which pushed up her tail feathers and exposed her vent opening.
>
> The insemination machine's job was to put a calibrated amount of semen into small plastic straws for the inseminator. The machine drew semen from a 6 cc. syringe and loaded the straws. With the tip of a rubber hose, the inseminator took a straw, inserted it in the

hen, and gave her a "shot." Then both men let go and the hen flopped away onto the floor. The breakers and the inseminator repeated this, bird by bird, until all the hens in the house had run through this gauntlet.

The semen came from the "tom" house. Here Bill extracted the semen bird by bird. He worked on a bench which has a vacuum pump and a rubber-padded clamp to hold the tom. From the vacuum pump, a small rubber hose ran to a "handset." With it, Bill "milked" each tom. The handset was fitted with glass tubes and a syringe body; it sucked semen from the tom and poured it into the syringe body. My job was to catch a tom by the legs, hold him upside down, lift him by the legs and one wing, and set him up on the bench on his chest or neck, with his rear end sticking up facing Bill. He took each tom, locked his crossed feet and legs into the padded clamp, then lifted his leg over the bird's head and neck to hold him. Bill had the handset on his right hand. With his left hand, he squeezed the tom's vent until it opened up and the white semen oozed forth into the sucking end of the glass tube. We did this over and over, bird by bird, until the syringe body filled up. Each one was already loaded with a couple of cubic centimeters of "extender," a watery, bluish mixture of antibiotics and saline solution. As each syringe was filled, I ran it over to the hen house and handed it to the inseminator and crew. (Mason, 1994)

Such treatment cannot be explained away on grounds of mere economic efficiency alone. It testifies to a hatred that humans have had for nonhuman animals through the ages, rooted in our hatred of ourselves for being animals, which we project onto them. In his book, *An*

Unnatural Order, Jim Mason calls this hatred of the animal misothery. Mason writes:

> I have coined the word misothery (miz OTH uh ree) to name a body of ideas that we are about to discuss. It comes from two Greek words, one meaning "hatred" or "contempt," the other meaning "animal." Literally, then, misothery is hatred and contempt for animals. And since animals are so representative of nature in general, it can mean hatred and contempt for nature—especially its animal-like aspects.

He continues,

> I deliberately constructed the word misothery for its similarity to the word mysogyny, a reasonably common word for an attitude of hatred and contempt toward women. The similarity of the two words reflects the similarity of the two bodies of attitudes and ideas. In both cases, the ideas reduce the power, status, and dignity of others. (163–164)

At the same time that humans experience misothery towards non-human animals and the "degrading" condition of animality, because we are animals and because the knowledge that we are animals is embedded in our biology and in our status as creatures rooted in the natural world, we are ambivalent. Hence, human misothery towards animals and the condition of animality may be considered "hypocritical" in the cautiously optimistic sense offered by Eli Sagan in his essay on aggression, in which he says that we must "treasure and expose that hypocrisy, because within it we will find the possibilities of further change" (110).

A basis for cautious optimism is the amity that many people feel for animals, which may be gaining ground on the animus that has distorted so much of our relationship with other species and nature, of which our treatment of the turkey in America is a prime example. Because of its mythic role in American history, the bird comes loaded with all of the ambiguity and "hypocrisy" that the role implies. Just as the wild ("sacred") bird and the domestic ("profane") bird join together ambiguously in the popular image and the DNA of the "Thanksgiving Turkey," so the bird is increasingly being placed in the role of ambassador of a more peaceful concept of Thanksgiving. In some cases people are adopting turkeys and treating them as guests at the Thanksgiving table,[6] showing, through a different set of symbols, that there may be other ways of saying thank you and exorcising guilt than by saying over and over again, "I'm sorry" (Pressley; Carton; Marshall).

However, this is a long way as yet from the mainstream, which officially considers the charm of a turkey to consist in the fact that the bird tastes good, while providing the easiest way to feel part of a community: by eating and saying what everyone else does. Otherwise, the turkey is considered a "dirty bird," addicted to filth and infected with harmful bacteria, that becomes magically clean only by being sprayed with acid, irradiated, cooked, and consumed (Nestor and Hauter, 23–26); a "stupid" creature that figures in the seemingly incompatible role of a sacrifice (a pure, precious offering), while serving as a scapegoat under the collective idea that heaping society's impurities onto a symbolic creature and "banishing" that creature can somehow bring purification.

Scapegoats are not just victims; they are innocent victims who are blamed and punished for things they are not responsible for. In the Mosaic ritual of the Day of Atonement (Leviticus 16), the scapegoat is "that one of the two goats that was chosen by lot to be sent alive into the wilderness, the sins of the people having been symbolically laid upon it, while the other was appointed to be sacrificed" (OED quoted in Girard, 73).

The Leviticus ritual is one example; the Greek *pharmakos* (a human scapegoat ritual from which the story of Oedipus derives) is another of a seemingly universal human phenomenon. In the Christian Bible, for example, Jesus is not only the Shepherd. He is the innocent Lamb who bears away the sins of the world. Concerning scapegoat rituals in the Western world, E. P. Evans writes in *The Criminal Prosecution and Capital Punishment of Animals*, "The ancient Greeks held that a murder, whether committed by a man, a beast, or an inanimate object, unless properly expiated, would arouse the furies and bring pestilence upon the land; the medieval Church taught the same doctrine, and only substituted the demons of Christian theology for the furies of classical mythology" (9).

In contemporary society, in secular terms now widely accepted, "the victim or victims of unjust violence or discrimination are called scapegoats, especially when they are blamed or punished not merely for the 'sins' of others, as most dictionaries assert, but for tensions, conflicts, and difficulties of all kinds" (Girard, 74).

Theoretically, scapegoats are not seen as such by scapegoaters, because scapegoating is not about evidence but about transferring blame. The role of recognizing a particular instance of scapegoating belongs to the "outsider," someone who sees the ritual from an unconventional standpoint, be it historical, cultural, subcultural, logical, or intuitive. In reality, people's perceptions of a scapegoat event of which they are a part may be more or less clear. The scorn heaped on the turkey at Thanksgiving shows a degree of uneasiness and defiance that indicates an awareness of scapegoating by those who practice it.

The idea of the Thanksgiving turkey as a scapegoat may seem like a parody of scapegoating, but what is the scapegoat phenomenon but a parody of reason and justice? The scapegoat, after all, is a goat. Animals have been scapegoats in storytelling, myth, and history every bit as much as humans, and probably more, as the scholar of myth and ritual, René Girard, observes in *Violent Origins: Ritual Killing and Cultural*

Formation. Social animals especially have been scapegoated since time immemorial. "[I]n all parts of the world," Girard says, "animals living in herds, schools, packs—all animals with gregarious habits, even if completely harmless to each other and to man," have been vilified (Girard, 86).

This is not simply a matter of other cultures and ancient history. Evans shows how the belief that "everything must be 'well-thought, well-said and well-done,' not ethically, but ritually" (36), contributed to the fact that until quite recently, European society hauled birds and other creatures before the bar in legal ceremonies as absurd as any scene in Dickens. "[E]xtending from the beginning of the twelfth to the middle of the eighteenth century," he tells us, the culprits were "a miscellaneous crew, consisting chiefly of caterpillars, flies, locusts, leeches, snails, slugs, worms, weevils, rats, mice, moles, turtle-doves, pigs, bulls, cows, cocks, dogs, asses, mules, mares and goats" (135–136).

Under European penal codes, "guilty" animals were subjected to everything from being buried alive to being burned alive to being hanged, often after mangling and other tortures were inflicted. Animals were put to the rack to extort confessions, and in classic scapegoat fashion, they were banished from the place of their alleged crime. (Evans, 138–139). Buggery, as we saw in Chapter 1 regarding the episode that took place in Pilgrim society involving turkeys and other farm animals, "was uniformly punished by putting to death both parties implicated, and usually by burning them alive" (Evans, 147), "so that the world was cleansed for good of evil" (Dekkers, 122). "Occasionally," Evans says, "an appeal led to the acquittal of the accused" (140). Considering this history, it is not farfetched to see the White House turkey pardoning ceremony as an inverted scapegoat ritual, a parody of a parody, burlesqueing "the acquittal of the accused."

So how, specifically, does the Thanksgiving turkey fit the scapegoat pattern? Consider that not all people are happy at Thanksgiving or Christmas as they're supposed to be (See Pleck, 37–38). Two cultures

coincide during the holiday season: the official, "pious" culture epito-
mized by *Life* magazine and the *Saturday Evening Post*, versus a miscel-
lany of dissident, unhappy, irreverent, and marginalized individuals
and groups, the two cultures being straddled by curmudgeons who
lampoon the sanctities from secure posts within the system. If a citizen
wishes to express discontent with "the day of guilt and grace, when the
family hangs over you like an ax over the sacrificial victim" (quoted in
Pleck, 37, who bizarrely calls this metaphor "that of the devouring
beast"), derision of the turkey comes in handy. This is the case when
Washington Post columnist Jonathan Yardley blames the "interminable
festive season" on the bird, who he says has "neither feelings nor taste."
Blaming the bird allows a certain amount of criticism and resentment
to seep into a celebration that *Life* magazine once said does not brook
angst or serious criticism ("Thanksgiving"), making Yardley's exactly
the kind of humor to which it is all right to subject Thanksgiving, since
it is at the turkey's expense more than the family's or holiday's.

The turkey thus functions as a bearer of impious sentiments
deflected from their true causes, like the obligation to be thankful,
whether one has reason to be thankful or not. Sorrow, death, suffering,
injustice—these are not the fault of the bird whose fate, after all, is to
be murdered for the meal, which is a cause of many people's great
unhappiness. But these negatives contradict how things are supposed to
be, how we're supposed to feel, and what may be properly expressed.
The person who wrote, "No meal can be sad" is wrong (Bakhtin, 283).
A meal made of misery makes many people both "nauseated and sad,"
as JoAnn Farb, a former poultry industry pharmaceutical company
employee (Davis, *Prisoned Chickens*, 19, 46–47), writes in her book,
Compassionate Souls (143). James S. Henry generalized his own feelings
in "Why I Hate Christmas." "To anyone who has ever been to a turkey
farm, Christmas and Thanksgiving take on a new and somewhat less
cheerful meaning," he wrote, (23).[7]

"For the Pueblo people, the turkey 'represents the Earth as fittingly as the eagle represents the sky....Being of and on the Earth, turkeys also became man's companion, both in life and in death' " (Christman and Hawes, 13). True or not, the turkey has not befitted from its association with human beings or been flattered by it. Humans would rather "fly like an eagle." Even the Pythagoreans aspired to forsake this earthly abode and ascend to a level of purity far above the earth's corruption (Porphyry, 11). Even for these classical ethical vegetarians and believers in the transmigration of souls, animals were considered the inferior companions of Man (Davis, "Savage Din," 148).

As a ritual scapegoat bearing a burden of sarcasm, the turkey fits into the carnivalesque tradition of taunting and torment stretching from Dionysus to Rabelais and beyond, in which "[a]ll that was terrifying becomes grotesque" (Bakhtin, 91). Opposite the sanctimony of pious occasions, the carnivalesque spirit emphasizes sarcasm, indecent abuse, the banquet, and a grotesque concept of the body (170–171). Its basic content is "[f]ree play with the sacred" (296) in which "medieval laughter" seeks to defeat fear in a "droll and monstrous form" (91). "[G]rotesque forms of the body," according to Mikhail Bakhtin in his classic study, *Rabelais and His World,* predominate in European art and folklore, especially in the comic genre. "[T]he theme of mockery and abuse," he says, "is almost entirely bodily and grotesque" (319).[8]

Just as the banquet and the grotesque body go together in the carnivalesque tradition, so the human body and other animal bodies are grotesquely mixed in it. The "transformation of the human element into an animal one; the combination of human and animal traits is, as we know, one of the most grotesque forms" of the carnivalesque style, according to Bakhtin. The traits involved are specific to the genre: beaks, claws, snouts, noses, phalluses, breasts, excrement, belching, bloatedness. Only the eyes, he says, "have no part in these comic images," because eyes "express an individual, so to speak" (316).

Nobody laughs at the Eagle. For impiety you have the Turkey. The turkey functions as the butt of marketplace humor opposite the sanctimony of the Thanksgiving celebration. The turkey is the grotesque body at the core of the Gargantuan feast, exhibiting those "physical and moral abnormalities" that have marked scapegoats through the ages (Girard, 105). In the media, the bird is a "humongous mutant" (Weiss, H1), a "winged behemoth" (Perl, 1995), a "chunko" (Yorke), a "fowl critter" (Schlesinger). Comparisons of the bird with sex symbols like Jayne Mansfield, Lana Turner, and Arnold Schwarzenegger (Colton, D13; Montgomery, B7); cartoons of little boys crawling into the turkey's vent at the Thanksgiving dinner table—"Send in small boy with a knife and instructions to fight his way out again" (Pearson); a postcard showing a smiling, aproned housewife holding the turkey's thigh stumps apart striptease style on her cutting board; a mocking personification of the turkey as a "gay" victim of society holding forth about his trials (Colton, D13); newspaper jokes about artificial insemination and the "sex life of a turkey" (Jones 1996, B2)—the entire panoply of derision bears out the prurient underside of Thanksgiving.

The modern bird's swollen body, distorted physical shape, and inability to mate naturally remind us not only of the cruel arbitrariness of fate, but of the sinister power of humanity (Fritz). The carnivalization of the turkey functions as a magic formula for conquering our fear of being a "turkey." We poke so as not to be poked at. By devouring another, we master our fear of being devoured. Today the fear of our own potential for gluttony, of being helplessly manipulated by the cosmic scheme, our fellow man, and our own folly has been transposed to the Comic Monster we are about to consume. A pathetic bird, conceived in the mind of Man, is purified and redeemed by being absorbed back into the bowels of Man. Theriomorphy, in which the human and nonhuman animal come together (Girard, 86), takes place under these circumstances in a consummation in which a creature otherwise maledicted as dirty and stupid undergoes transmutation. The profane animal becomes the sacred feast. Such is the Harvest Festival of the carnivalesque universe. "The victorious body receives the defeated world and is renewed by the very taste of the defeated world. Man triumphs over the world, devours it without being devoured himself" (Bakhtin, 281, 283, 285).

The Thanksgiving turkey ritual has all the trappings, including the "happy ending," of the traditional scapegoat ritual, in which a "culprit" is transformed into a benefit to society (Girard, 97). "People like to eat 'dumb' animals," a journalist writes, "critters for whom they can muster little sympathy....However, when properly prepared, they [turkeys] taste really good" (Hall, 1995, 4).

> Warning. This carcass contains dangerous bacteria that can make you sick and even kill you, your mother or your child. Do not eat raw. Do not touch with bare hands. If turkey "juice" drips on your fingers, call the hospital immediately or contact the Turkey Hotline at 1–800–DEATHWATCH. Stock your kitchen with an arsenal of antibacterial liquids and sprays. Cook thoroughly. Keep away from small children. Wear gloves. Throw them away. Slaughterhouse workers lose their fingernails and their hands turn black from handling turkey bacteria and blood. Their arms discolor and they break out in bumps. Sometimes the skin peels off. Parsley, sage, bacteria, and thyme. / Decontaminate your kitchen at Thanksgiving time. / Detox the turkey before you dine (Cook, 78–79; Goldoftas, 27; White).

The consumer newsletter *Moneysworth* sounded all the familiar notes in its 1973 article "The Light and Dark Sides of Thanksgiving

Turkey," including the scapegoaters' self-portrait as "the passive victims of their own victim" (Girard, 91).

> Things to know about the pea-headed bird you are about to consume. Your dinner was an obese, immobile thing, hardly able to stand, much less fly, a sort of feathered Jayne Mansfield, including the massive stupidity of such women. You are about to eat an antibiotic-ridden bird raised in conditions so squalid they have raised the spectre of an Andromeda Strain of bacteria in animals becoming resistant to antibiotics and then being transmitted to humans as untreatable, incurable diseases. Are you concerned that your demand for bloated meat has caused the poultry industry to use methods that may harm you in order to comply? (Like the arsenical acid they put in your turkey's food?) Don't worry: say your blood cholesterol is high. Soak a couple of yards of cheesecloth in butter or margarine and drape it over the bird. And remember, whatever happens to you, it's the turkey's fault, not yours. Only consider that some of these narcissistic mutations become so hypnotized by their reflections as they drink the water in their filthy sheds that they drown themselves. Sadly, it might be better if some of the birds that reach your table had been drowned rather than slaughtered to serve you. (See Cook, Goldoftas, and White)

Actually, if they live long enough, these birds do get to be drowned in an electrified water bath, a scald tank, and a chill tank at the slaughterhouse, which for one food editor has "all the elements of a car wash, fun house and circus in one."

There's the water—it's everywhere—spraying from small nozzles and big hoses, or surging around in giant-sized chilling tanks. It's on the floor, on the birds, maybe even dripping on your head.

Then there's that scary fun-house sensation: You're not sure what loud noise or ugly object might come at you next. And then there are the birds, who look like tired trapeze artists, swinging limp and upside-down from shackles as they move continuously through the plant.

Dunk, spray, drip. Another conveyer line of turkeys just went through Shady Brook's special rinse—Assur-Rinse, it's called. During their 12-second trip, the birds travel partially immersed in yellowish bubbly water through a narrow stainless-steel basin. At the beginning of the brief bath, their exposed drumsticks get sprayed with the rinse; another nozzle sprays Assur-Rinse into the cavities.

The birds come out sopping wet, so their flaccid necks are yanked to drip them dry; then they get showered again with plain water. Next, they dive together (yes, of course they're dead) into the chilling tanks—giant swimming pools of chlorinated water that reduce their body temperature quickly so bacteria cannot grow. But their dunk in the pool can exacerbate cross-contamination, meaning that if one carcass is contaminated with salmonella now others may be. (Sugarman, 1994b, E1, E11)

This is the carnivalesque spirit plus a reminder to decontaminate your kitchen and have a stock of antibiotics in case of food poisoning, although "[t]he more we use antibiotics, the more bacteria evolve into forms that resist them" (Brownlee). This is because many of the same antibiotics that are used to fight food poisoning from handling and eating contaminated birds are being used to fight the bird diseases that make people sick who eat the birds. The joke about the Thanksgiving turkey moldering long after the meal is over is true in more ways than one: "The thing about Thanksgiving dinner is, it lingers" (Yardley).[9]

If "unanimity [is] indispensable to the correct performance of sacrifice" (Girard, 100), the days of unanimous deprecation and contagious consumption of the turkey may be numbered. The bird is a kind of test case. Either "eating meat is fun," as a journalist said in an interview (Hall, 1998), or "eating meat is mean," as a child told her mother why she would not eat turkey at Thanksgiving (Eisner). The question posed by Native American author Michael Dorris concerning America's persistent cruelty to Native Americans applies to our treatment of that other group of native Americans involved in our history: "Is it necessary to the American psyche to perpetually exploit and debase its victims in order to justify its history" (Dorris, 6)?

Philosopher Peter Singer places this question in a broader perspective of intellectual inquiry. He writes:

> I have likened reason to an escalator, in that, once we start reasoning, we may be compelled to follow a chain of argument to a conclusion that we did not anticipate when we began. Reason provides us with the capacity to recognize that each of us is simply one being among others, all of whom have wants and needs that matter to them, as our needs and wants matter to us. Can that insight ever overcome the pull of other elements in our evolved nature that act against the idea of an impartial concern for all of our fellow humans, or better still, for all sentient beings? (1999, 62–63)

Such is one philosopher's way of "talking turkey" about what we as a society and a species may be capable of achieving in the realm of social progress and justice.

---

1. Deep pectoral myopathy: a condition in which the chest muscle tissues die, leading to strangulation of the blood vessels within the muscle. In breeder turkeys this is due in part to the birds' "struggling and wing beating associated with catching for artificial insemination" (Pattison, 19, 229).

2. As with Canada geese and white-tailed deer, excuses for killing manufactured overpopulations of turkeys spilling into suburbia and elsewhere are already in place. See Sterba on the "mixed blessing" of the turkey comeback, including "people–turkey interface, or trouble. In eastern Montana, ranchers complain of turkeys breaking into their hay bales in winter....In suburban Boston last spring, a postal worker in Danvers reported carrying a broom to ward off turkeys pecking at his tires and threatening him on his route" (A6). On May 3, 2001, a Minnesota state trooper intentionally drove his squad car over a female turkey befriended by residents in the Minneapolis suburb of Chaska, claiming the bird endangered public safety. See Collins.

3. See Pearce's 1999 article "Gobbling Up the Grand Slam" for more on the female turkey hunter. There, a daughter joins with her dad to "collect" a bird from each subspecies. That's the "Grand Slam."

4. " 'Electro-ejaculation isn't as efficient as hand massage,' explains [Annie] Donoghue, a reproductive physiologist whose official objective is to improve turkey reproduction.... The lab turkeys, she goes on, are "trained" to respond to a "milker" stroking his [the turkey's] tail feathers in a suggestive manner. 'The turkeys are very, very calm and unruffled throughout the procedure,' Donoghue reports....'It's almost like they line up sometimes. Some of them hang around afterward, hoping for a second chance, I guess' " (Jones 1996, B17).

5. ConAgra is the largest turkey processor in the U.S. and the country's largest meat seller. See Schlosser, *Fast Food Nation*, 158–160; and the Sierra Club's 2001 report, *Spoiled Lunch*.

6. Farm Sanctuary's Adopt a Turkey Project, begun in the 1980s, launched the media-friendly practice of including rescued turkeys in an all-vegetarian Thanksgiving, resulting in dozens of newspaper articles each year.

7. In Elizabeth Pleck's otherwise pertinent discussion of the "postsentimental Thanksgiving [that] emerged in the 1960s" (37), among the dissident groups and reasons for dissatisfaction with the holiday Pleck cites, there is no mention of the sizable and seemingly

growing number of people alienated by the slaughter of forty-five million birds for the holiday season (Philip, C16).

8. See Pleck, 30–33, on the "carnival-like celebration of Thanksgiving" in America dating from the 1780s to the 1930s, rooted in "the raucous English celebrations in the fields." Pleck rightly notes Bakhtin's approval of carnivalesque humor and carryings on but fails to clarify the elemental animus of the carnivalesque spirit. Its jollity consists of hostile-aggressive malicious mirth, the opposite of good-natured heartiness and fun. The carnivalesque spirit is antirevolutionary. It does not challenge the System but operates securely within "official culture," upholding it in the manner of, say, Jay Leno and *The Tonight Show*.

9. For a documented discussion of the link between food poisoning, animal agriculture, antibiotics, and animal products, see Nicols Fox's book *Spoiled* (1998). By the 1970s, Fox says, the Centers for Disease Control (CDC) "noted a truly significant jump in *Salmonella* infections every November. The obvious association was the Thanksgiving Turkey" (154).

6 ~~~

RITUALS OF SPECTACULAR HUMILIATION

An Attempt to Make a Pathetic Situation Seem Funny

An attempt to make a pathetic situation seem funny.
—Jim Mason, *An Unnatural Order*, 257

He observed the huge crowd and noted that some of the wildly flapping gobblers were able to escape capture temporarily by darting under wagons, horses, and mules.—Kuykendall and Howard, "Turkey Trot Day at Oliver Hall's Store," 113

It was a big day for the town, and always covered by the media. In the article I read in the Alabama Review, *there was no voice of dissention against the cruelty that the turkeys were being subjected to. Today, we have a different sort of ceremony, which is offensive on a more sublime level.*—Katy Otto, "The Truth Behind the Pardoning Ceremony," 5

The justification for these kinds of events is always that the animals don't mind because they are dumb.—Alaister Highet, "Turkey Contest at Inn Opposed," 7

I N DECEMBER OF 1989, THE *NATIONAL ENQUIRER* DID an exposé of a festival tradition in Yellville, Arkansas known as the turkey drop (Blosser and McCandlish). That coverage, with its photographs of turkeys in mid-air being dropped from airplanes, put an end to the town's official sponsorship of the turkey drop. However, pictures speak louder than words only to an extent. Journalistic cues—attitude and interpretation—are crucial in determining how a mass audience will respond to graphic depictions of certain kinds of cruelty such as the turkey drop. In this instance, the *Enquirer* deplored the "nightmarish scenes" of turkeys being thrown from moving aircraft a thousand feet above the ground, plunging through the air at fifty miles an hour, crashing, and being chased down, cornered, and captured by local youths.

Through the years, the *Enquirer* explained, turkeys subjected to the Yellville turkey drop have slammed into power lines, telephone polls, office buildings, and trees.

> One turkey slammed into a power line so hard the wire bent down about three feet before snapping back up. The bird hit the ground, shocked and dazed, and tried to walk...pitifully trying to run on two obviously broken legs before it was crushed to death by a pileup of kids....After smashing into a tree and coming to rest on a branch, one of the birds was pursued by a gang of kids who captured and fought over it—using it in a grisly tug-of-war that ended when one boy tore the turkey's wing off.

The turkey drop was the highlight of Yellville's annual October Turkey Trot Festival, sponsored by the Chamber of Commerce. Festival chairwoman Janie Purdom told the *Enquirer*: "We have a wonderful festival. Each year we also drop 10 to 12 wild turkeys from a plane. Townspeople gather below and try to catch one to take home and eat. We LOVE turkeys! The festival is to recognize the wild turkey, a popular hunting bird throughout Arkansas."

However, the *Enquirer* called the turkey drop "sick," a "bizarre Arkansas celebration," and a "Festival of Death." These words, together with the photographs, produced such an outcry around the country that the Yellville Chamber of Commerce cancelled its sponsorship of the turkey drop (Purdom). Had the *Enquirer* chosen instead to represent the turkey drop as a "charming" or "quaint" American tradition, it might still be going on.

A similar entertainment took place in Collinsville, Alabama, which each year held a "turkey trot," along with the more ominous sounding "turkey drop." In the turkey trot, derived from driving turkeys to slaughter on foot, as discussed in Chapter 4, Collinsville residents chased turkeys, chickens, ducks, and geese through the streets with brooms and other farm and household implements. According to the *Alabama Review*:

> Turkey Trot Day at Oliver Hall's store in Collinsville in DeKalb County in northeast Alabama was held annually the day before Thanksgiving from 1912 through the mid 1930s. The brainchild of Irby Hall, the colorful, innovative elder son of the store's founder, the event brought crowds of 8,000 to 10,000 people to a town of only 700 residents to watch the release of turkeys, guineas, chickens and geese....
>
> Crowds gathered around Hall's store and on roofs of adjoining buildings, with some of the more daring men and boys stationing themselves in nearby trees and on telephone poles. The appearance of Sol Kerley, an elderly black employee of the Halls, signaled that action was to begin. Wearing a tall, silk top hat, the black man climbed to the roof of the store where stood a scaffold approximately twenty-five feet high. A springboard about ten feet long extended from the scaf-

fold over the street. With an air of authority the master of ceremonies cracked a buggy whip to force various sizes and colors of fowl to walk the plank and with a long pole prodded those unwilling to fly.

The turkeys usually fluttered into the air, soared for short distances, and then skimmed just over everyone's head before tiring and dropping into the crowd. Following a frantic crush of people with outstretched arms, feathers flew, and some jubilant farmer emerged with his prize. (105, 108)

While the pictures in the *Alabama Review* are almost as appalling as the ones in the *National Enquirer*, the writers treat the Collinsville turkey trot and drop as a colorful American festival tradition. Turkeys trying desperately to balance themselves on telephone wires after being dropped head down from a scaffold are said to be performing "acrobatic stunts" (112). The authors give no hint that there was anything wrong with treating the birds this way.

Anthropomorphic victimization of animals in the form of recreational rampages against them has been "medicine" for human society through the ages. In England, for example, in addition to the football games, wrestling matches, and cudgeling contests that took place on calendar holidays throughout the year, traditional male activities also included bull-baiting, bull-running, badger-baiting, bear-baiting, dog fights, cockfights, cock-throwing, and other animal-abuse sports. As Robert W. Malcolmson notes in *Popular Recreations in English Society 1700–1850*, "Human beings, it seems, have always had a strong disposition to manipulate animal life for 'sporting' purposes" (45). For example, he quotes an 18th-century description of cock-throwing, which consisted of hurling cudgels and broomsticks—"scails"—at roosters tied to a stake, an activity that was part of the pre-Lent saturnalia of Shrovetide (Mardi Gras),[1] the carnival season:

[O]n Shrove Tuesday the most unmanly and cruel exercise of cock 'scailing' was in vogue everywhere, even in the High Church 'lighten' and many other places in the city and in the country. Scarcely a churchyard was to be found but a number of those poor innocent birds were thus barbarously treated. Tying them by the leg with a string about 4 or 5 feet long fastened to the ground, and, when he is made to stand fair, a great ignorant merciless fellow, at a distance agreed upon and at two pence three throws, flings a 'scail' at him till he is quite dead. And thus their legs are broken and their bodies bruised in a shocking manner...and wonderful it was that men of character and circumstance should come to this fine sight and readily give their children a cock for this purpose." (Malcolmson, 48)

Cockfighting was already established in England by the time the Romans took over in the first century CE. "There is nothing more diverting," according to an 18th-century enthusiast (Malcolmson, 50). Rituals of violence based on animal abuse, such as cockfighting, have frequently been justified as being not only acceptable outlets for human aggression; they have been sentimentally defended as social levelers in which Men of All Ranks could join together in a common enterprise etched in "the inner recesses of the masculine psychic life" (Smith and Daniel, 124). Whatever else might have brought men together on English social occasions in the past, according to Malcolmson the "common denominator was particularly noticeable in the practice of animal sports" (67).

In *An Unnatural Order: Uncovering the Roots of Our Domination of Nature and Each Other*, Jim Mason identifies two basic types of animal abuse entertainment: "rituals of spectacular violence" and "rituals of spectacular humiliation." These rituals overlap; but in terms of emphasis, whereas rituals of spectacular violence "reinforce myths about vicious animals and evil nature," rituals of spectacular humiliation "reinforce myths of animal stupidity, inferiority, and willingness to submit to human domination" (253). Viewed thus, cockfighting is a ritual of spectacular violence, the circus is a ritual of spectacular humiliation, and rodeos manifest the convergence of both types of ritual. Ironically, those who defend these rituals will insist that those who oppose them are anthropomorphizing animals.

A good example of a modern animal abuse ritual of "spectacular humiliation" was the so-called Turkey Olympics. In this carnivalesque sport held in a New England town, turkeys were taunted and mocked them as a warm up for Thanksgiving Day. The Turkey Olympics was an annual Saturday-before-Thanksgiving event sponsored by the Inn at Lake Waramaug in New Preston, Connecticut from 1978 to 1997. It was mainly local until November 24, 1993, when Fox aired it on national television. From then on, a campaign led by the national animal rights organization United Poultry Concerns sought successfully to put an end to the Turkey Olympics, which was permanently cancelled in 1997 (Highet 1997, 1).

Previously, the inn issued coy press releases, as in the following excerpt from its 1990 announcement:

> Arriving in the latest fashion of turkey sweatbands, running shorts, t-shirts, and head bands it is quite obvious these turkeys have come to the Inn to win. There will be a few choice athletes provided by the Inn On Lake Waramaug for those whose turkeys missed the qualifying round....
>
> Pure hysteria ensues with several 50-foot long racing heats on a well manicured 12 lane track. The winner takes home the Gold Medal of Gobblers, a wreath of Indian corn. Other events include the high jump,

the giant slalom, a race to see which turkey can eat a bowl of feed the fastest, and the heaviest turkey competition. (Kane)

Others saw the Turkey Olympics differently:

We saw a pen full of "supplied" turkeys set up for those who had reserved a bird for the occasion. People went into the pen, picked out a bird, forced the bird into a costume, and brought the costumed creature out to the cheering crowd. Some turkeys had to be held by several people at once in order to force on the costume. People were in a raucous mood, with lots of drinking.

Turkeys were knocked about, pushed, and threatened with sticks. They were carried in their costumes out into the arena—"Mu-Donna," "Fred Flinturkey," "The Big Kahuna." The MCs mocked them. "Here comes 'Turkey Sandwich.' " Turkey Sandwich was pushed through the 50 yard dash. The ultimate low was a bird plucked from the pen and labeled "The Turk-A-Nator." Dressed in camouflage and emboldened with Budweiser, the people behind this stunt showed off their big bad bird riding in his own custom tank wearing a black cape. As he was pushed down and held firmly in his killing machine, a woman marched beside the "warrior" with a large placard showing a killer turkey that said:
TURK-A-NATOR
Possible Resume
  Pluck You
  I'm Foul
  I'll Be Baked

Eat My Stuffing

I'm Fried

Two busloads of mentally and physically challenged people were brought in for the day. Many children were there. Feathers were strewn about where birds had been forced into costumes, made to run and jump, and had even been ridden. Some birds in the holding pen pecked at each others' neck feathers. Some birds were bleeding. (Kelly, Letter)

The sponsors of the Turkey Olympics insisted that the games were not cruel because turkeys are "not clever," they were going to be eaten anyway, and the about-to-be-slaughtered birds used in these games were "not substantively harmed by a little fun and exercise" (Highet 1994, 1). Invoking the usual formula for these types of recreational cruelties, they said it was "just a fun day, a traditional day." "Turkeys are people, too." "Some of my best friends are turkeys" (Highet 1994, 7).

In its editorial pages the *Hartford Courant* agreed that the "annual Open Turkey Invitational" was "sophomoric," but claimed to be shocked that so many people should rally to the cause of birds with a reputation as "low achievers on the pecking order" bred to be eaten ("Show some respect for turkeys"). Who could read with a straight face, the paper asked, a letter to the editor which said that by standing up for turkeys we "increase the amount of moral courage in the world"?[2]

However, enough people openly objected to the Turkey Olympics to get rid of it, just as enough people objected to the Turkey Drop in Yellville, Arkansas and got rid of that, too. It required national exposure obtained through animal rights pressure to force the sponsors of the Yellville Turkey Drop and the Turkey Olympics to take notice.[3] It took the eyes of "outsiders" to put these cruelties in a light that those who defended them refused to recognize or could not see.

Those same outsiders witnessed yet another turkey-abuse ritual of humiliation and death, this one conducted in the woods of Schuylkill County, Pennsylvania. Sponsored by the Lone Pine Sportsmen's Club, outside the town of Middleport, the event was a live turkey shoot in which approximately one hundred leg-bound turkey hens from a nearby farm were shot at for recreation (Hindi 1995a). The undercover video footage shows a group of men and one woman binding up the legs of these birds and plunking each one down on a rubber tire in the woods. After smoothing down the birds' feathers as if tenderly, they proceed to shoot them. In the forty-five-minute tape derived from several hours of footage obtained on June 11, 1995, you hear guns being fired at hens by shooters you can't see, and you watch bullets slamming into the ground in front of hens up close to the camera, showering dirt in their faces. Sometimes a hen panics. Mostly, however, the birds sit still with their heads held high and their eyes wide open, leg-bound in the tires.

Time passes, *Pow*. You watch a hen get hit. You watch her die. *Pow*. You watch another hen jerk, bounce from the tire, tumble and bump like a rock down the grassy rubble. She's alive, but her legs are tied, so she bumpity-bumps along until she comes to a stop. If we imagine the scene from another perspective, the sport goes like this. They tie your hands behind your back, and they tie your feet together. Then they set you down in a junkyard tire out in the woods. The woman—the "Maenad"—comes over and smoothes down your hair. She studies you a bit, then pats you on top of your head. Then she kind of smoothes your shoulders down and moves on. We watch you sitting in your tire. Your eyes are open, you move your head a little, but mostly you just sit there, stiff, with your neck and head up. *Pop*. You're hit. Down the hill you go, all balled up, rock-tumbling along. You roll to a stop and struggle. Now the same woman who smoothed you down a few minutes ago comes over to you with her hatchet. She bends over you and casually starts hacking at your neck with it. However, something else gets her attention, and she walks away. You've been shot (perhaps by her), your neck is half off, you're tied up, and you're alive, and she walks away....

Live turkey shoots in which turkeys are set up as opposed to being shot at in trees go back at least as far as colonial times. According to the Oregon Department of Fish and Wildlife, live turkey shooters bound the turkey—"concealed its body in some way—either by putting it in a box or by staking it behind a log—so that its head was free to bob around" (Stahlberg, 5D). The turkey's bobbing head was the target. Colonial shooters fired a single musket ball at the bird.

According to the National Wild Turkey Federation, the colonial turkey shoot was "extremely challenging." It was a "marksmanship competition using a live target the size of a 50-cent piece, at a pre-set distance, probably about 60 yards. With open sights and with a target that was moving, needless to say it was extremely difficult" (Stahlberg, 5D).

Live turkey shoots began to die out around the turn of the 20th century, when the destruction of wild turkeys and their habitat had rendered the birds nearly extinct. Today, the term "turkey shoot" refers to a gun-club sponsored competition based on shooting at clay pigeons or paper targets, with frozen turkeys as prizes. Otherwise, it is called a "live turkey shoot," a more clandestine affair.

In the case of the Schuylkill County turkey shoot, the tape was given to the news media, and the TV tabloid *Hard Copy* did an exposé of the shoot on December 4, 1995, along with the Hegins Pigeon Shoot—the Labor Day sport of Schuylkill County that put Hegins on the map until 1999 when the Pennsylvania Supreme Court ruled against it (Hulsizer v. Labor Day Committee, Inc.).

Even before the media got hold of it, the Lone Pine Sportsmen's Club president was begging the animal rights group CHARC (Chicago Animal Rights Coalition), which conducted the investigation, not to distribute the turkey shoot tape in exchange for the club's promise to stop sponsoring the shoots. The gun club's president reportedly told

CHARC's president, Steve Hindi, that he himself had begun to feel that the shoots weren't right. One way or another, the gun club didn't want the publicity, but they got it anyway (Jordan, 1995b).

---

1. For a glimpse of modern day Mardi Gras, see H. Scott Jolley, "Chicken Run," *Travel and Leisure*, February 2001.
2. Quoted from my letter of November 30, 1994.
3. The Animal Protection Institute of America, based in Sacramento, CA, led the successful campaign against the Yellville, Arkansas Turkey Drop.

7

IGNOMINY, THY NAME IS TURKEY[1]

The Presidential Pardoning Ceremony

I am the turkey. Each year you select one from my species to receive the poor honor you have devised: a photo session with your president. This is our paltry reward for having passed into your language as a synonym for stupidity. You hope it will distract us from the gleeful carnage you call Thanksgiving. The ceremony is a sham and I have come to say so.—Jim Naughton, "The Turkey Ritual: Stuff It!"

Tomorrow, 45 million turkeys will make the ultimate sacrifice for America's feast. But not this one. I'm granting this turkey a permanent reprieve. After many years in the coop, he's on his way to a farm in Virginia to bask in the sun, collect his hard earned pension, and enjoy his golden years. And that's one less turkey in Washington. (Laughter.) Happy Thanksgiving. (Applause.)—President Bill Clinton, National Turkey Pardoning Ceremony, The White House Rose Garden, November 26, 1997

In certain French cities a custom was preserved almost to our time to lead a fatted ox through the streets during carnival season. The ox was led in solemn procession accompanied by the playing of violas.... The ox was to be slaughtered; it was a carnivalesque victim. It was a king, a procreator, symbolizing the city's fertility; at the same time, it was the sacrificial meat, to be

chopped up for sausages and pâtés.—Mikhail Bakhtin,
Rabelais and His World, 202

Q. *"Anthropologists tell us that in the past, certain cultures have
asked forgiveness from animals being hunted for consumption.
How does the turkey 'pardoning' idea fit into this scheme?"*
A. *"It doesn't fit into that at all. We're not asking for forgiveness.
They are not an endangered species."*
—Stuart Proctor, president of the National Turkey
Federation. Interview with Katy Otto

AT FIRST GLANCE THE PRESIDENTIAL TURKEY
pardoning ceremony is a far cry from the rituals we've been
looking at. It does not take place in a backwater or the back-
woods or go roaring down Main Street. The presidential turkey isn't
chased with a broom, dropped from a plane, forced to run races, or tied
up among the trees and shot at for sport. The dead body isn't used as a
bowling ball to feed the hungry (AP, 1994). The ceremony is held in
the White House Rose Garden in the nation's capital, surrounded by
an audience of underprivileged schoolchildren selected from
Washington, D.C.'s inner city.

Where the turkey pardoning ceremony differs most notably from
the previous rituals is in the lack of overt physical harm done to or
intended towards the bird during and after the ceremony. The turkey
is placed on a table, wearing only talcum powder (Colton, D1). He
may be patted but not poked by the thirty or so invited guests. The
turkey is "pardoned," not sacrificed, in a mock-magnanimous gesture
performed by the President of the United States. This bird, together
with his "back-up," in case something goes wrong, gets to live out his
life in a display pen at a visitors farm in suburban Virginia following
his fame.

What is the purpose of the pardoning ceremony? According to Julie DeYoung, a spokesperson for the National Turkey Federation, the industry's trade group since 1939,

> the overall purpose has been twofold. One, to lead as a kick-off to the Thanksgiving holiday and provide an opportunity for the president to present a holiday message to the nation, and obviously from our perspective it's to raise the visibility of the turkey industry and its contributions to the American economy, to the role that the turkey industry and all of agriculture play in feeding the American public. It's very positive, it's something that all of the presidents seem to enjoy doing, so it's a fun thing to do. It's really to celebrate the holiday and heighten the visibility of the industry to the American public. It seems to be a real win-win. It gives the White House an opportunity to give a positive mesage to the public. It's a nice photo opportunity. (De Young, 446)

In a way, it was the turkey pardoning ceremony that inspired this book. The ceremony brought into focus material I'd been gathering for years and putting in folders ranging from "Artificial Insemination" to "Zoonotic Diseases." I soon had enough clippings to create a folder for "Negative Views." Eventually, the turkey pardoning ceremony branched into a folder of its own. I studied photos of U.S. presidents surrounded by a corps of Babbitt-y looking men and one or two women grinning over a massy white lump on a platform or scrambling to grab hold of a blur of feathers pounding heavily off the platform.

I have clasped such heavy turkeys in my arms enough to know what it feels like when they fall, or are about to fall, which is almost worse. I've watched their panting die down with a palpable sense of a heart attack barely postponed. I know the open-beaked, eyes-wide-open, chest-heaving, trying-to-avoid-suffocation look of the fragile behemoth struggling to regain his equilibrium. These are not old turkeys either; they are not even a year old.

Contrary to what the media say, Harry Truman was not the first U.S. president to "pardon" a turkey at Thanksgiving (Sowell). When I first started looking into this ceremony, I expected to find a full-page black and white photograph of President Truman pardoning a turkey in *Life* magazine in 1947, the year the ritual supposedly began. But there was nothing, not even about Thanksgiving. On December 16th, the *New York Times* noted under "Amusements," page 46, without any pictures, "President Truman today received his Christmas turkey—a 47-pound champion. Caged in a red, white and blue crate, the big bird was presented to Mr. Truman by A. E. Matlack of Ramona, Calif., president of the National Turkey Federation, and officials of the Poultry and Egg National Board" (AP).

In November 1948, President Truman received seven turkeys from various groups, including a "dressed champion" from the Poultry Science Club of Ohio State University. He said he was going to eat this one on Thanksgiving Day (AP). At Christmas that year, Truman was photographed in the *New York Times* with two live turkeys: a bronze one along with one of the new white Beltsville, Maryland laboratory turkeys created by the U. S. Department of Agriculture "for small apartment-dwelling families with small ovens." Truman "chucked them under the chin and the birds flapped their wings vigorously, giving the cameramen some action shots" on the back porch of his office. Truman said that the birds, donated by the National Turkey Federation and the Poultry and Egg National Board, would "come in handy" to feed twenty-five people at his Christmas dinner ("Turkeys for the President's Christmas Dinner"). During his presidency, Truman received a number of turkeys at Christmas, but they were meant to be eaten, not saved, or "pardoned."

The presentation of a live turkey at Thanksgiving started under President Eisenhower. It was a presentation, not a pardoning, and it did not always take place. In 1953, the president of the National Turkey Federation said he would have the turkey—a badly debeaked, open-mouthed tom tweaked on the dewlap by Eisenhower wearing his famous smile—"killed, frozen and returned to the White House" (AP). Two years later, in 1955, Vice President Nixon accepted a bird for Eisenhower. According to the papers, this bird was destined for Eisenhower's Thanksgiving Day table in Gettysburg, Pennsylvania (AP Wirephoto).

In 1956, a man from Reno, Nevada urged "General Eisenhower" to "lead the nation in a humane Thanksgiving" by putting the presidential turkey "in a coma before killing him" ("President Gets a Turkey and Plea to Use Mercy"). It may thus be assumed that no "pardoning" of a turkey was yet in place, since a pardon is normally considered more humane than a coma.

To this day, the "humane coma" idea has not been adopted in the United States for any of the 268 million or so turkeys slaughtered each year (USDA/NASS). Two years after the man from Reno proposed a humane coma for the presidential turkey, the 1958 "Humane Methods of Slaughter Act" was passed, excluding all poultry, including turkeys—a situation that has never been changed.[2] Clearly, the General did not lead this charge.

The closest thing to a Thanksgiving turkey pardon prior to President Reagan was when President John F. Kennedy "spared" the life of the turkey he received in 1963, saying, "We'll just let this one grow. It's our Thanksgiving present to him" (AP). The turkey was presented to Kennedy wearing a gold ribbon that said "Good Eating, Mr. President" with the "usual" frozen turkey in the wings. Though at first Kennedy told the press he intended to keep the bird, he then announced that the bird the press called "too large for a normal oven" would be returned to the farm it came from to be used for breeding.

This, in fact, is part of what the pardoning ceremony is all about: "The White House birds can't be pardoned because they're not intended to be eaten in the first place" (Yorke). Turkeys destined for whole bird consumption are slaughtered at around four months old. The males weigh thirty pounds or less, and the hens weigh half as much, including their feathers. In contrast, the White House turkeys are of breeding stock age. They are always males, they weigh an average of fifty pounds, and they are between six and twelve months old (DeYoung).

Male birds are used because they are bigger than the females and provide an opportunity for more fun. "I don't think anybody says this out loud but we joke about how each year's chairman [of the National Turkey Federation] tries to top the previous year's chairman by bringing a bigger and bigger turkey, much older than the turkey you would buy in the store to eat and the turkey that is served" (DeYoung).

Accepting the bird in 1970, President Nixon declared, "I can't use this bird. Look at those eyes" (UPI). However, there is no mention of what happened to the bird after the ceremony. As late as 1977, the Associated Press reported that Vice President Mondale, acting on behalf of President Carter, "accepted a live 51-pound Thanksgiving turkey...destined for the White House dinner table." However, this is unlikely. Doubtless the bird went straight to the slaughter factory where, according to the National Turkey Federation, breeding-size birds "are processed for what are called canner packs—that is, they are going into soups or stews, things that are already cooked where the tenderness of the meat isn't quite as important. And also, as you said, pet food and other byproducts, animal feed" (DeYoung).

It was during the 1980s that the presentation evolved into the pardoning ceremony it officially became in 1989, the year George Bush took office in the wake of the Iran-Contra scandal surrounding his immediate predecessor, Ronald Reagan. That year, Bush announced that the White House turkey the *Washington Post* called "big and stupid" was being "granted a presidential pardon as of right now" (Sherrill, C1–C2). (Bush later issued pardons to six Reagan administration officials who had either been convicted or indicted, or stood to be indicted, in the Iran-Contra scandal.)

Under Reagan, both the bird and the Rose Garden pardoning ceremony became primary vehicles for political satire linking the White House with the turkey as a symbol of the carnivalesque politics of the Iran-Contra scandal. As a former movie actor now on the political stage, Reagan was well suited to conducting the ceremony.

In 1977, Vice President Mondale joked about a turkey he said once splashed a Senator with excreta in order to get the Senator's attention (AP). In 1981, the year Ronald Reagan took office, Reagan told a turkey carving joke and a "turkey plane" joke, and held an exchange of double-entendres in which he kidded the president of the National Turkey Federation that he knew plenty of turkeys—here he turned to the bird—"But you're the real thing" (Reagan).

In 1987, the ceremony played like a bristling parody of a Greek drama complete with a mocking chorus and a somewhat vulnerable but tough and elusive protagonist king. As soon as the "nearly comatose" bird, "Hawaiian Charlie" (named for the National Turkey Federation's first president, Charles Wampler, and an upcoming NTF convention in Hawaii), was brought into the Rose Garden, the press started yelling, "Is that turkey sedated?" "Did that turkey just say no?" "How long has that turkey been dead?" (Williams 1987, D9).

> Q. What's going to happen to that turkey?
> Ms. Range [Deputy Assistant to the President and director of public relations]. He's going to a pet farm.
> Q. Mr. President, are you going to pardon North and_____?
> The President. So, you can say happy Thanksgiving right in front of him, and it doesn't matter. [*Laughter*]...

Q. Are you going to pardon North and Poindexter, sir?...

The President. If they'd given me a different answer on Charlie and his future [that he was going to live out his life at a pet farm], I would have pardoned him. [*Laughter*] ...(Reagan 1987)

Thus, while the Ronald Reagan Presidential Library says that Reagan "did not use the term 'pardon' in regard to the turkey during the 1987 presentation" (Fletcher), indirectly, he did. He used the word pardon in the same way that he used the White House turkey on that occasion, as an ironic reference to an uncomfortable political situation. The press patronized him as he sought to end the ceremony ("Listen, I have to go back_____"): "Stroke the turkey one more time." "Just give it a parting stroke, sir." "Atta boy!" (Reagan).

If the press couldn't get a rise out of Reagan, it forced one from his familiar; one of them goosed Hawaiian Charlie's genitals (Williams 1987, D9). (Three years earlier, in 1984, in order to get an action shot, photographers prodded "R.J." with clucks and gobbles, causing him to leap off the platform ("Reluctant Guest at White House Ceremony"; "Guess Who's NOT Coming to Dinner"). In 1988, the president's double was parodied in the *Washington Post* bemoaning his fate, year after year, as the object of a "mocking chorus of 'gobblegobblegobble-gobbles' "[?] and other indignities (Naughton). But this, the *Post* said later, was precisely the role of the White House turkey and his "understudy"—"our reigning national symbols of Thanksgiving and turkey-tude" (Trueheart, B6).

In 1989, the year George Bush turned the presentation into an official "pardon," thirty inner-city schoolchildren were invited to the ceremony (Sherrill, C2), a practice that continued under President Clinton. Why not use lower-income children to present a kinder image of America, similar to the way "an older black man was used to throw the bird off a platform by his employer at the old Collinsville, Alabama Turkey Trot ceremony" (Otto, "Truth"), or the way handicapped people were busloaded in to watch the Turkey Olympics?

In "The Truth About the Pardoning Ceremony," Katy Otto, a University of Maryland student who interviewed National Turkey Federation representatives in 1998, speculated on the White House's use of poor children and minorities for the ceremony: "It is important to examine how the exploitation of animals can be linked to the exploitation of human beings, especially minorities. It seems ironic that the specific group of poor children chosen to attend the ceremony would be the one that would reflect well upon the Capitol Hill staffers, and that the National Turkey Federation has such a plush office in the corporate part of Northwest Washington D.C. in contrast with how a lot of people are actually living in the poorer parts of D.C. This is a marked contrast to the land of the free the National Turkey Federation was describing to me."

When NTF spokeswoman Julie DeYoung told Otto that the trade group considered it "educational" for these youngsters to see where their food came from, Katy "asked how exactly the children could learn where their food is coming from by seeing a live bird which is going to be kept at a petting zoo. She [DeYoung] said that it shows them that there is another stage besides the grocery store."

What happens to the birds after the ceremony? According to the *Washington Post*, "[B]etween the new people at the White House and the new people at the Turkey Federation, no one seems to even know where Hawaiian Charlie, the 1987 bird presented to President Reagan, went. Bob Johnson, owner of Pet Farm Park in Vienna [Virginia], vaguely remembers taking in R.J. (short for Robust Juicy) after his 1984 White House visit. 'He was robust all right. He was so fat that he couldn't even walk. He died before Christmas. I mean, he was really a chunko!' " (Yorke).

At least one of the birds sent to Kidwell Farm at Frying Pan Park in Northern Virginia, where they've been going since 1989 (Yorke) died of "foot rot," according to the *Washington Times* (Bedard, A9). This is not surprising considering the filthy, untended mudyard the two birds I saw in September of 1997 were living in. Though the place has been spruced up since then in response to my complaint to the Fairfax County, Virginia Park Authority (Davis, letter to James A. Heberlein; Heberlein, letter to author; Baldino, letter to author), according to the *Washington Post*, neither the presidential turkey nor his back-up pardoned in 1999 "saw their 18th month. The second one keeled over by summer's end" (Montgomery, B7).[3]

I put the question about the meaning of the pardoning ceremony on the Internet and got back the following replies. Brian Luke, a philosopher, said that the ceremony makes sense if we understand Thanksgiving as a sacrificial blood ritual and the turkey as the communal sacrifice eaten in the manner of antiquity to unify society. By designating a common sacrificial victim, we ritually constitute ourselves as a nation, a role that is also played by war. We are the sacrificers, turkeys are the ones sacrificed, which is why the government tries hard to insure that every citizen, from the indigent to the institutionalized, gets a bite of turkey over the holiday, and why most people can't accept turkeyless Thanksgivings. "It is the community all partaking in the flesh that unites everyone."

At the same time, modern industrial society has become so alienated from the food production process that people can easily forget that an animal had to be killed in order for the turkey to get to the oven. Consequently, all kinds of articles, cartoons, jokes, and bizarre rituals crop up right before Thanksgiving, emphasizing the subjectivity of the bird. That way we can't miss the fact that someone—a turkey, not a turnip—had to be sacrificed for the feast. "By pardoning one turkey it becomes obvious that all those other millions of turkeys Americans are eating were not pardoned."

In Luke's opinion, the pardon is also "a display of power that connotes the power that presidents and governors have to pardon criminals, including those sentenced to death, a display of male power in particular. In traditional societies it is always men who cut animals' throats to ritually sacrifice them. The cutting shows the power that men exercise over domesticated animals and that they may also exercise over human groups that are similarly unable to defend themselves. This veiled threat is reproduced in modern industrialized America through the Thanksgiving tradition of the man of the household carving the turkey. The cutting displays the threat. Selecting a victim to be spared reinforces it."

Deborah Tanzer, a psychologist, agrees, noting that it is important to recognize the levels of awareness at which such motives generally operate. "The cultural pressure to have everyone eat even a bite of turkey for group cohesion at Thanksgiving works in large part through the unconscious," she says. "The displays of power involved in killing turkeys, 'pardoning' turkeys, and carving turkeys need not be consciously seen as displays of power, or felt consciously as intimidating threats, but in no way does this preclude their being experienced as such unconsciously, which is the (again largely unconscious) cultural aim. Like symbols generally—myths, metaphor, poetry—such rituals aim for the unconscious and impart their message there."

Another correspondent felt that these interpretations read too much into the ceremony. The President "pardons" a turkey "because little kids (and adults) have been entertained by it and to kill the bird might upset some youngsters or parents. It is the 'kind,' or proper, PR thing to do, just as some radio stations have 'pulled' plans to kill turkeys on the air." Most men these days, said the correspondent, have little connection with the bird. "I've seen women carve turkeys, I've seen men. In either case, I don't think anyone interprets the cutting of meat, bread, or vegetables as any kind of 'threat' or indication of power.

I think that most people don't consider the suffering or bloodshed of the turkey. It is just another food product" (Patty).

Batya Bauman, a feminist animal rights advocate, feels that the above viewpoints are not incompatible. The latter, she argues, is a more immediate response, whereas the first two represent "a different kind of analysis that draws on atavistic and mythic precedents, in which the sacrificial slaughter of and feeding on turkeys is part of the historic question of why we humans behave the way we do."

If such behavior is an innate part of our species, the fact that we can identify and analyze it is of itself no guarantee that we will ever eliminate the behavior or experience any universal desire to do so. If we are in the process of becoming conscious of what we are doing so that we can no longer justify the collective violence of animal sacrifice as a matter of unconscious choice, but desire to do it anyway, then we can expect that a self-consciously dismissive rhetoric will continue to dominate the discussion, as it does now.

An example is Peter Perl's 1995 article in the *Washington Post Magazine*, "The Truth About Turkeys," where he says:

> Okay, before we go any further, let's talk turkey: Vegetarians and animal rights activists may not like this story. They think it is morally wrong to kill, eat or even confine anything that had a mother. Actually, meat-eaters may not be able to stomach this story either, because they would rather not know too many intimate details about the personal lives of animals on their strange and terrible journey to that last roundup in the Meat Department.
>
> Me? I say lighten up. I am, like most Americans, a committed carnivore and will eat all kinds of meat— except road kill, unless it is well-seasoned and served with an appropriate wine. I also say, like most

Americans, that food animals should be treated humanely on their way to a humane death, which, I believe, is very big of me. (16)

As might be expected, Perl singles out a particular turkey for symbolic exemption from "the last roundup in the meat department." Sam II is the pet (hence, already "pardoned") of a couple that raises and slaughters turkeys for Thanksgiving. He is a member of a class of rare breeds known as Bourbon Reds:

> Then I walked over to the private domain of Sam II, who was roosting on a wood plank five feet off the ground inside his personal 8-by-8 coop. I couldn't help but marvel at how warlike he looked with his curved beak and multicolored coat, and how spry he was, pacing back and forth on his roost. By contrast, his commercial turkey brethren could not have even gotten off the ground, let alone walked a narrow plank. I called and gobbled at Sam II and suddenly, with an awesome fluttering of his wings, he swooped down to the ground, raising a cloud of dust and feathers. I was amazed to see him take off, and before the dust could even settle, Sam II leaped right back up to his roost, a proud turkey in flight.

1. Trueheart, B6.

2. The three bills introduced in the House of Representatives by Congressman Andy Jacobs from 1992 to 1995 were defeated in the House Agricultural Subcommittee on Livestock, Dairy, and Poultry: H.R. 4124, H.R. 649, and H.R. 264. See Davis 1993c; and Davis, 1996d, 122–124.

3. "Pardoned" turkeys started being sent to Northern Virginia "pet farms" in 1982 ("Singled Out"). In 1984, the turkey and (perhaps) his backup went to the Pet Farm, and from

1985 to 1988, to Evans Farm (Yorke; Reagan, 1988). Since 1989, they've been taken to Frying Pan Park, in Herndon, Virginia.

8

THE MIND AND BEHAVIOR OF TURKEYS

The male is credited with a somewhat greater mental capacity than the female. No one will claim that either has much intelligence.—A. W. Schorger, The Wild Turkey, 146

The apologies that precede discussions about wild turkey intelligence are definitely not warranted. I have never observed another animal making such a dedicated effort to know and to understand.—Joe Hutto, Illumination in the Flatwoods, 162

I have been involved with many thousands of chickens and turkeys and I don't think they are good pets, although it is evident that almost any vertebrate may be trained to come for food.—Thomas Jukes, a poultry researcher. Letter to the author[1]

Turkeys are often described as stupid, because of the difficulty they display in adapting to life in commercial flocks. Young birds may starve, unable to locate food and water....In their natural state, turkey hens show strong maternal instincts, caring for and teaching their young how to cope with life's challenges. All modern turkeys are artificially hatched and most are pitched into the bleak environment of a huge shed at an early age. The expression 'fussing like a mother hen' has become part of our vocabulary. Turkey mothers are equally protective. Most

young animals learn from their parents, and behavioural prob-
lems can result from unnatural conditions and maternal depri-
vation.—Clare Druce, *Hidden Suffering*, 23–24

THE INTELLIGENCE OF BIRDS IS A RELATIVELY NEW area of scientific interest and investigation compared to that of mammals. Dogs, whales, dolphins, and the great apes—chimpanzees in particular—as well as pigs, have been studied, and, not surprisingly, various claims have been made as to which species of animal among them is the "smartest."

Among birds, in addition to Konrad Lorenz's pioneering ethological studies of geese, jackdaws, and other birds that engaged his patrician intellect, the intelligence of pigeons attracted significant scientific interest in the 20th century due to their homing abilities and their use as messengers in war (Schlein, 26–34). Pigeons demonstrate an astonishing ability to handle complex geometrical, spatial, sequential, and photographic concepts and impressions, to solve all kinds of complicated problems, retain precise memories, and invent ways to communicate their understanding, intentions, and needs to human beings. Lesley J. Rogers's book, *Minds of Their Own*, summarizes pigeons' conceptual feats in laboratory tests that I personally would fail, and can hardly follow (30, 66–69, 71–72).

More recently, investigator Irene Pepperberg has highlighted the intelligence of parrots, based on her years of laboratory experiments designed to elicit an array of cognitive responses from Alex, an African Gray parrot, from the correct use of human verbal language to complex discriminations among shapes, colors, objects, and relationships (Rogers, 1995, 218; Moore; "Bird Brain"). It may be assumed that these experiments, which treat Alex rather more like a kindergarten child than an adult creature, barely hint at Alex's or any other normal parrot's true range and specific nature of intelligence, but they may be a step in the right direction.

I say this in part from having lived with a blue-fronted Amazon female parrot for over twenty years, until she died. Once, when she—Tikhon—and I were living together in San Francisco in the 1970s, we visited a bird rehabilitator whose house was filled with owls, hawks, and other injured species. Despite his proximity to all these birds, the rehabilitator insisted that birds are not very intelligent, but are bound, regardless of evidence to the contrary, by "instinct." Rogers describes a similar situation in *Minds of Their Own*, in which a scientist who demonstrated cognitively complex responses in pigeons, including self-awareness, perversely insisted that "if a bird can do it, it cannot be complex behaviour and it cannot indicate self-awareness of any sort" (30).

Fortunately, the tide is shifting, and birds are beginning to be vindicated after a long reign of denigration and ignorance of their nature and mental capacities. For this, we can thank people like Irene Pepperberg who have held firm in a frequently resistant scientific environment (Rogers and Kaplan, 72). All of this doesn't count for a whole lot yet, since even to be a nonhuman animal on the highest level of cognition within the current universe of thought—a chimpanzee or a whale, for example—is to be a poor contender according to our standards of value: the vaunted chimpanzee ranks rhetorically with "intellectually disabled human beings" among those pressing for an upgrade in their status from property to personhood (Singer, 1994, 183), and rights for great apes as a group are being promoted on a basis of their having the minds of children (Wise, 267–270). Such comparisons are not only unjust but absurd. Unimpaired adult animals embody such a repertoire of experiences accompanying their growth, including practical decision-making, that it is nonsense to equate it with the experiential repertoire of children and the cognitively disabled.[2]

While current evidence suggests much more than merely "that some birds display signs of intelligence" (Orlans, *et al.*, 263), still, parrots and pigeons, along with crows, wrens, woodpeckers, kingfishers, finches, seabirds, and others are now being acclaimed for their hitherto undreamed of cognitive capacities. For instance, it used to be assumed that birds were locked into responding only to the immediate moment, without any sense of before and after. But, as Alexander F. Skutch shows with many examples in his book *The Minds of Birds*, "Birds are aware of more than immediately present stimuli; they remember the past and anticipate the future" (13).

In particular, the ground-nesting birds known as galliforms ("cock-shaped") were traditionally denigrated by Western science as stupid "[i]n spite of their fine feathers" (Schorger, 70). Chickens, turkeys, pheasants, quails, peafowl, guinea fowl, and a host of other birds believed to have a common ancestor were dismissed without further ado as "unquestionably low in the scale of avian evolution" (70). Among scientists, this assumption has been challenged and may even be said to have been debunked. For those interested in what is now scientifically known and inferred about the minds of chickens and of birds generally, I refer readers to Lesley J. Rogers's books, *The Development of Brain and Behaviour in the Chicken* and *Minds of Their Own*, and Rogers and Kaplan's *Songs, Roars, and Rituals: Communication in Birds, Mammals, and Other Animals*.

Rogers, an avian physiologist, says that the information obtained from the research she cites "is beginning to change our attitudes to avian species, including the chicken" (Rogers, 1995, 213). Significantly, she states that "[w]ith increased knowledge of the behaviour and cognitive abilities of the chicken has come the realization that the chicken is not an inferior species to be treated merely as a food source" (213), and that "it is now clear that birds have cognitive capacities equivalent to those of mammals, even primates" (217).

Although turkeys are not mentioned in it, *The Development of Brain and Behaviour in the Chicken* discusses many different kinds of birds from which inferences about turkeys may reasonably be drawn.

Wild turkeys appear in Alexander F. Skutch's book, *The Minds of Birds*, in company with the chicken, the ring-necked pheasant, and the Mallard duck, as examples of the ability of "downy, open-eyed preco-cial chicks, which leave their nests within hours or at most a few days of hatching and follow their parents," to distinguish the voice of the parent or foster parent from other hens' voices, even when the parent is deliberately kept out of sight (3–4).

In *The Human Nature of Birds: A Scientific Discovery with Startling Implications*, Theodore Xenophon Barber includes the domestic turkey, albeit briefly and inadequately (106–107). The power of Barber's book consists in his enthusiastic argument on behalf of birds and in the wealth of anecdotal evidence he presents, much of it in the form of quotations from ornithologists, artists, and writers, concerning indi-vidual birds and neighboring flocks whom these people evoke with verve and precision. Unfortunately, Barber's brief section on "poultry" lacks the spark, cogency, and keen observations that elsewhere enliven this book.

It is one thing to state, as Barber does, that domesticated chickens and turkeys have been bred for fast growth, large size, and "meaty" breasts. It is quite another to say that they have been bred for "minimal intelligence," that they "do not act at all like natural birds," are "virtu-ally desexualized," are missing "a significant part of their instinctual intelligence," and "cannot live without the assistance of humans" as a result of diminished mental capacity (107). Ignored as an insuperable cause of these birds' dependency is the fact that they are grossly over-weight and out of proportion and are thus unable to walk fast or fly into trees. They are inclined to lameness, respiratory congestion, mat-ing infirmities, and heart disease, and most have white feathers that prevent them from camouflaging themselves. Blanket assertions about diminished mental capacity in domestic fowl fail to take into account, as well, the documented success of feral chickens and turkeys (Schorger, 144–145; Nicol and Dawkins, 46).

Sanctuary workers such as myself, who have spent years in the company of turkeys and chickens bred for the meat industry, know that these birds have not been desexualized or reduced to minimal intelligence. The inability of male turkeys to mate properly does not reflect a loss of their desire to do so. Rather it results, as can be seen by watching them repeatedly and unsuccessfully trying to mate, from the growth disorders imposed on them, added to the fact that in all likelihood their claws and part of their beaks were cut off at the hatchery. In addition, they are frequently in orthopedic pain. Poultry scientist Ian Duncan writes, for example, that "evidence of anatomical studies show that adult male turkeys of large body-weight lines suffer from degenerative hip disease which causes enough pain or discomfort to reduce spontaneous activity markedly and to interfere with sexual performance. These findings suggest that the welfare of males of this strain at one year of age is poor" (203).

As for their intelligence, the ability of domesticated "meat-type" chickens and turkeys to respond alertly and appropriately to sensory and social stimuli, and to negotiate the physical, social, and emotional milieus in which they find themselves, say, at a sanctuary or in an adoptive home, indicates considerable intelligence, awareness, and learning potentials in these birds. If Sarah, a former battery-caged hen, climbed the stairs in the morning to get me downstairs to fix her breakfast after yelling from the bottom of the steps failed to produce results, was she not displaying purposeful adaptive intelligence? And what about Katie the "broiler" hen, who pecks at my pant legs to get me to bend down and hug her?

Rather than showing that chickens and turkeys are stupid, the fact they become lethargic in continuously unstimulating commercial environments shows how sensitive these birds are to their surroundings, deprivations, and prospects. Learned helplessness, which may as well be referred to as "learned hopelessness," is a pathologic adaptation of living beings to pathogenic living conditions from which they cannot escape. Children warehoused from their infancy in institutions and wild animals forced to spend years behind bars undergo similar apathy and atrophy of body and spirit. The psychology of this condition is insightfully discussed in John Berger's essay "Why Look at Animals." It was illustrated dramatically in human beings in the 20th century by sensorially deprived Romanian orphans, whose plight of lifelong institutionalization was highlighted on the television news program *Turning Point* ("Romania").

In the case of chickens and turkeys reared motherless on factory farms, in buildings in which the dimensions of time and space are reduced to monotonous extensions of toxic waste devoid of comfort, colors, and novelty, and which are filled with thousands of sick, dead, and dying birds stretching along a floor farther than the eye can see, it must never be forgotten, as Lesley Rogers states in *The Development of Brain and Behaviour in the Chicken*, that "cognitive capacity depends on environmental stimulation throughout development, even on stimulation of the embryo" (219). Thus, for example, writes Rogers, "it would not be sufficient to take a battery reared hen and compare [her] with, say, a jungle fowl raised in more natural conditions" (219).

A few years ago, a study was undertaken at Oregon State University to learn the extent to which people's acceptance of Darwinian evolution of physical form included an acceptance of Darwinian evolution of mental form as well. The study, which focused on student and faculty perceptions of domesticated animals, was published in 1998 in the *American Society of Animal Science*, under the title, "Do Domestic Animals Have Minds and the Ability to Think? A Provisional Sample of Opinions on the Question" (Davis and Cheeke). In the study, as described by the authors,

> [f]aculty, staff, and graduate students in a number of departments, students in an undergraduate course, and some groups outside the university were polled to

obtain their perceptions about whether domestic animals have minds, the ability to think, and differing degrees of intelligence (the surveys focused only on horses, cows, sheep, dogs, chickens, pigs, cats, and turkeys). A clear majority of all groups surveyed (except the Department of Zoology) said yes, they believe animals have minds, but a substantial number of those in animal sciences and zoology (17 to 25%) said no. A number of others in animal sciences, zoology, and philosophy (11 to 37%) refused to answer the question because the concept of mind was not defined. From 80 to 100% of respondents in other groups said yes to the question of minds. From 67 to 100% of all participants said yes, they perceive that animals have the ability to think, but a substantial number of animal scientists, zoologists, veterinarians, and English faculty said no, animals don't think (6 to 33%).

On the question Do domestic animals differ in relative intelligence?, the responses varied from 88% in animal sciences to 100%. Surprisingly, when asked to rank different animal species by intelligence, there was a remarkable degree of similarity across all groups regardless of background; the overall ranking from highest intelligence to lowest was dog, cat, pig, horse, cow, sheep, chicken, and turkey (2072).

Except for the pig, the animals fell unremarkably into two groups, with companion animals in the top group and farmed animals in the bottom group, reflecting stereotypes of farmed animals versus "pets" in the United States. According to the authors, "[O]ur books, teachers, entertainment, and so on portray dogs as having the highest intelligence and turkeys as having the lowest" (2076).[3]

While a certain number of those polled complained that the concept of mind was not defined in the survey (deliberately, according to the authors), no one seems to have questioned the idea of ranking the intelligences of animals in the first place, supporting the claim by Peter Singer (and others), whose own anti-speciesist philosophy nevertheless consists of ranking humans and nonhuman animals according to a hierarchy of their entitlement to "personhood," that "the existence of a hierarchy or system of rank is a near-universal human tendency...deeply rooted in our human nature" (Singer, 1999, 37). In this poll, rankings of the comparative intelligences of the animals in question reflected, in the authors' words, "a phylogenetic scale suggested (concluded) at least decades ago with primates at the top, followed by dog, cat, elephant, pig, horse, birds, and so forth" (2078).

How Intelligent are Turkeys?

Disparagement of the turkey's intelligence has been taken to task by the American naturalist and wildlife artist, Joe Hutto. In his book *Illumination in the Flatwoods: A Season with the Wild Turkey*, Hutto describes how he incubated two clutches of wild turkey eggs (sixteen and thirteen each) that had been abandoned by hens disturbed off their nests by tractors on a quail hunting plantation in the North Florida flatwoods. In the tradition of philosophic naturalists such as Henry David Thoreau and Loren Eiseley, Hutto puts his keen observations of natural phenomena in a speculative cosmic perspective. In the form of a daily log suffused with meditation, Hutto trains his eye and that of the reader on the orphaned wild turkeys he incubated, tended, rejoiced with, and agonized and mourned over from May 1991 into the following year, by which time most of the birds had either died, been killed, or disappeared.

Hutto recounts the birth of his turkeys, and because their birth is an amazing event that most people are unaware of, I have chosen to

give in full the emergence of the first turkey from its shell as recorded
by its "mother":

> May 10, Friday
> At 5:00 P.M. I enter the incubator for conversation and
> notice a small hole in the upper surface of one egg in
> clutch #2. A small hole, the size of a pinhead, but on
> close examination I see the movement of what appears
> to be the tip of a tiny wild turkey bill. I turn off the fan
> in the incubator, and as I talk to the eggs, I can hear
> faint peeps coming not only from the pipped egg but
> distinctly from others as well. In fact, as I speak softly
> and make soft yelping sounds, a small chorus of peep-
> ing wells up from the eggs, and then slowly dies down,
> as if they had grown tired....
>
> Eventually the pipped egg becomes active again.
> Three hours have passed since I first noticed the activ-
> ity in this egg. I turn off the fan and begin talking and
> making light yelping noises. The little turkey responds
> with peeping and attacks the eggshell with a bite on the
> shell and a movement of the head that he repeats in the
> same way over and over again. Gradually, a uniform
> line begins to develop that seems to be confined to a
> particular latitude, approximately one-third of the way
> from the larger end of the egg. The hatching activity is
> punctuated with rest periods lasting only a minute or
> two. Often, it seems that he resumes hatching in
> response to my vocalizations. At last, the end of the egg
> falls away, hinged by only a small piece of membrane.
> The little turkey pushes at the door he has created and
> scrambles free of the egg. The entire process has taken
> fifty-five minutes.

This new arrival struggles awkwardly with his new-found freedom. He is wet, and gravity seems to be pulling in every direction while an untested equilibrium attempts to establish the correct placement of head and feet. For a moment the little wild turkey lies motionless and helpless, striving to catch his breath. I remember to make a sound. Speaking very softly, just above a whisper, I make a feeble attempt to console him in what seems to be a desperate and confusing moment. Instantly, he raises his shaking wet head and looks me square in the eyes. In that brief moment I see a sudden and unmistakable flash of recognition in the little bird. Something completely unambiguous transpires in our gaze, and I am certain that the young turkey absolutely knows who I am. I am totally disarmed as the little creature struggles across the towel, never interrupting his gaze, and eventually presses himself against my face, which awaits him at the edge of the shelf. Gradually, he makes himself comfortable, his peeps and trills subside, and I realize that something has also moved inside of me. (19–20)

From Hutto we gain an enormous amount of information about developing young turkeys such as we can obtain elsewhere about them, only Hutto transforms the language of documentation into a kind of lyrical drama sharpened to the pain of a pinpoint at times. We learn that a clutch of turkey eggs is about twelve, that the birds are well developed inside the egg for a considerable time before hatching, and that their fetal vocalizations are audible to the hen, who responds to them in turn. We learn that the average hatching time for a clutch of eggs is twenty-four hours (25), that drying time on hatchlings is six to eight hours (21), and that, before they can stand, newborn turkeys will aggressively peck at anything small and outstanding as presumably or potentially edible (22).

A captured insect is shaken by the poult until dead, and then eaten. Poults protect their captured prey while siblings chase them for it and try to grab it out of their beaks, indicating an innate sense of possession and jealousy from the earliest age (Hutto, 25). According to wildlife biologist William M. Healy, this comical "grab-run" behavior in young turkeys also has "the practical effect of transferring information about food sources among flock members" (65).

Newborn turkeys, like other gallinaceous birds (including chickens, quails, and pheasants) are, to the human eye, Hutto writes, "irresistibly cute." Baby wild turkeys are "very round and are covered with a thick, soft down, broken up into patterns of dark brown distributed over a field of dull yellow. Their bills are pale in color and are capped by the little protuberance called the egg tooth, which assists in the hatching process and is shed in a day or two. The legs and feet are a light brownish pink. The eyes are dark brown, almost black, and very intense" (22).

For Hutto, the eye of the turkey is the focal point for drawing attention to the bird's ability to negotiate the world in which it finds itself, including bonding with others. Relating to Hutto as their parent, the poults "prefer it eye to eye" (56). At just over a week old, though they still "sleep in a single pile" at night (37), Hutto's birds are not only capable of flying; they show a confident visual awareness that "at once includes the smallest crawling particle on a leaf and the red-tailed hawk soaring a half mile up the field." At eight days old, they are "already developing the thousand-yard stare" (45). When a possum comes snooping into their pen one day, perhaps to make an easy meal, and Hutto chases it off, he looks back and sees the watching poults "standing together, each very tall and silent" (45).

Hutto spurns what he calls the "mythology of misunderstanding" surrounding turkeys that presumes a lack of intelligence in the birds to compensate for our own lack of understanding of them (72). Examples arc the turkey's notorious difficulty with see-through fences and the notion that young turkeys will stand with their beaks up and drown in the rain.

The young turkey's tendency to squeeze into tight places anticipates the ease with which adult birds can wedge their way through thick vegetation with their heads, which are particularly small compared to their overall body size. Their small head, aided by their thick, glossy, armor-like feathers, enables them "to slide silently and effortlessly through" thickets (72). A wire fence, which they can see through but not walk through, is alien to the turkey's evolutionary experience. Turkeys glide so easily through tangled vegetation that they become frantic when the wires, unlike vines, won't "give." In my experience, the domesticated turkey glides with the same or similar ease through tangles and thorns I can't shove my bare hand into. When, for example, our turkey hen Priscilla became broody, she would lay her eggs in places impenetrable to me. Once or twice, until I knew better, I thought she was trapped in a tangly thicket and tried to lift her out, but she appeared to be "stuck." Only, she wasn't! She sailed out of the density when she decided to, as if the "sea" parted at her will.

Turkeys do not stand there and drown in the rain, Hutto insists. The apparent basis of the notion that they do is that when it rains, turkeys seek to make their overhead silhouette as small as possible in order to reduce their overall exposure to getting wet. They do this by streamlining themselves, raising their head and neck, keeping their body erect and their tail down. Hutto calls this the turkey's "rain posture" (73). Young turkeys deprived of the opportunity to dive under their mother's wings may die of chill when it rains, he says, covered as they are with down, but they don't drown. When I asked my sanctuary assistant Holly Taylor about this, she said that if young chickens and turkeys occasionally drown in the rain it's because they instinctively look up to see what is falling on them, and in doing so their noses can clog quickly with water if no one is there to shelter them fast enough, as in nature the mother bird would do.

Much has been made of the commercialized domesticated turkey poult's "stupidity" in the huge sheds into which they are dumped motherless after having undergone partial beak amputation and the removal of their toenails at the hatchery just after birth. The turkey industry concedes that the newborns are traumatized by the amputations and other harsh treatments they receive upon hatching. According to an article in *Turkey World*, "Poults come in one side of the service room bright eyed and bushy tailed. They are squeezed, thrown down a slide onto a treadmill, someone picks them up and pulls the snood off their heads, clips three toes off each foot, debeaks them, puts them on another conveyer belt that delivers them to another carousel where they get a power injection, usually of an antibiotic, that whacks them in the back of their necks. Essentially, they have been through major surgery. They have been traumatized. They don't look very good" (Donaldson, *et al.*, 27).

Young turkeys need their mothers or a comparable foster parent. Wild turkey poults are as dependent on a mother or parent substitute as their domesticated counterparts are to get a proper start in life. Unlike baby songbirds and raptors, whose parents are absent for long periods gathering food to take back to their young in the nest, it is unnatural for gallinaceous birds such as turkeys, who live with the hen from birth and for four or five months thereafter, to be separated from the parent (Hutto, 61). As noted in *The Wild Turkey: Biology and Management*, "Hens have a remarkably long association with their poults....Although poults have innate responses to some objects, it is clear they also learn from the hen" (Healy, 59). She is "the center of the brood flock, and vocal communications keep the poults in orbit around her" (57).

The relationship between the hen and her poults during the first three to four weeks when poults require brooding includes the poult's panic on becoming separated from its mother, causing it to emit a loud and insistent *peep peep peep* which in subsequent weeks becomes a coarse and desperate cluck. Hens, Healy writes, "are always socially dominant over poults" (58), but they do not necessarily lead the flock's daily activities. They may lead or follow, "responding appropriately to the calls of poults and to other stimuli." In his observation,

> If a poult began peeping, the hen would increase the volume and rate of yelping. If peeping continued, the hen would move toward it. Hens would run toward shrieking poults. As poults became tired or cold, they would give low-volume peep calls. Hens would respond by pausing and calling. If several peeping poults approached, the hen would crouch to brood and poults would come to her. (58)

As Lesley Rogers in *The Development of Brain and Behaviour in the Chicken* does regarding young chickens, so Healy stresses the importance of the bonding between the poults and their mother in the normal social development of turkeys. He notes that long association with the hen "seems essential," and that the process of "hatching eggs in incubators and raising poults in mechanical brooders interrupts social experiences that are the foundation for normal adult behavior in wild turkeys," including parental behavior (60). He points out that much of what is known about the wild turkey's intelligence is based on work with domestic turkeys (46), whom he semi-defends from the charge of stupidity by observing that given genetic selection for "such gross breast development that few adult males can even walk, let alone breed," it is "not surprising that such creatures are considered stupid" (65).

People have become so used to seeing photos of turkeys of uniform age and sex crowded inside a shed awaiting their death that it's a shock to learn about the lively poults and their mothers chasing

grasshoppers in a meadow, sunning themselves (Hutto writes beauti-
fully that wild turkeys are "composed of a large proportion of sun-
shine" which they "gather"), and dustbathing together, leaving "tiny,
bowl-shaped impressions the size of small wild turkey bodies" (34).
Turkeys young and old shake the earth from their feathers as refreshed
as a person after a water bath. Dustbathing, by which turkeys, chickens, and many other birds practice bodily hygiene, is also related to
the annual replacement of feathers in birds known as molting, which
"appears to produce an itching in the skin" to which frequent dustbathing gives relief (Schorger, 177).

As noted, the mother is the center of the young birds' universe.
Hutto says that a lost young wild turkey will go to any turkey he or she
sees, but given a choice the bird will always join its group, which "as a
whole will then faithfully seek the parent" (89). A delightful picture of
the wandering hen and her slightly older brood, including an errant
youngster, appears in Schorger:

> They hurry along as if on a march to some particular
> point, sometimes tripping along in single file, one
> behind the other, and at other times scattered through
> the woods for fifty yards or more. When on these scat-
> tered marches it is pleasant to note some straggling
> youngster as he wanders out of sight of the main flock
> in an attempt to catch a fickle-winged butterfly, or
> delays by the wayside scratching amid the remains of a
> decayed log in search of a rich morsel in the shape of a
> grubworm....[W]hen he discovers that he is alone...[h]e
> raises himself up, looks with his keen eyes in every
> direction for the flock, and, failing to discover them,
> gives the well-known coarse cluck. Then he raises his
> head high in the air, and listens intently for his moth-
> er's call. As soon as it is discovered that one is missing

the whole flock stops, and the young turkeys raise their heads and await the signal from their mother. When she hears the note of the lost youngster, she gives a few anxious "yelps," which he answers, and then, opening his wings, he gives them a joyous flap or two and with a few sharp, quick "yelps," he goes on a run to join his companions. The march then continues with all busy picking a morsel here and there, and scratching away as busy as bees among the leaves and brush in search of bugs and worms. They continue their march through the day and generally wind up in the evening somewhere in the vicinity of their roost of the preceding night, very frequently at the same place when not disturbed. (Quoted in Schorger, 283–284)

For the first four or five weeks, the young birds sleep on the ground under the hen's protection. Then they leave the ground "and fly, at night, to some very large low branch, where they place themselves under the deeply curved wings of their kind and careful parent, dividing themselves for that purpose into two nearly equal parties" (Audubon quoted in Schorger, 284). So far removed are most of us from this scene that the picture on the cover of this book of a turkey hen roosting on a tree limb surrounded by her poults not infrequently raises the question, "What kind of a bird is that?"

Just as pigeons generalize from familiar objects to novel ones—witness their successful "leap" to tall city buildings and window ledges from their native cliffs and rock ledges—so domesticated turkeys search for and make use of objects in the human environment that allow them, for example, to roost above the ground at night. About the only thing that stops them from perching is their weight and accompanying disabilities. Boris, our male turkey, was grounded by his infirmities, which killed him before he was two years old. But Florence, our female turkey, often sleeps on a bale of straw at night, or else she perches on the lid of the large can the birds' food is stored in.

Over the years I have frequently watched adult white "meat-type" chickens and turkeys calculate a leap onto a perch, be it a roosting board, a fence top, a bale of straw, or a sawhorse. They will test the spring from the ground before actually making it, as if reliving an experience built into their bones and brain cells. They will revise their position, test it again, and quit if they perceive it's no go, with a show of disappointment and frustration, often circling the area with their necks craned before giving up entirely. However, if they can perch, they normally will. The turkeys that Healy writes about selected the largest trees and roosted as high as they could. Their determination to perch "was so strong that it was difficult to keep human-imprinted turkeys out of the tops of trees in our pens even by clipping all the flight feathers on one wing. The turkeys would climb leaning branches and leap from limb to limb to get into tree crowns and then gradually work their way to the top" (62).

The turkey's humorous image is primarily based on the courting behavior and sexual characteristics of the adult male bird during the spring mating season. His body language announces both season and mood, and his face and head fairly burst with red, white, blue, and mulberry colors during this time. It is no surprise that a species as preoccupied as ours is with symbols and fantasies about sex would have a priapic reaction to a bird so primordially and passionately male at this time of year. The bird gobbles from the treetops at the beginning of spring and at dawn to call the females and signal the males, hallooing his "lordly morning roll" so as to make the very tree trunks reverberate with the sound of all the gobblers shouting at once (Schorger, 151). He struts and emits a "pulmonic puff" and low humming drum around the females as a prelude to mating, and is filled with fury or fever depending upon which sex he is seeking to impress. His sexual condition blazes in the enlargement of his wattle, which hangs like a necklace of marbled red pearls from his throat down the front of his chest, and in the swell and increased length of his snood that, starting above his beak, goes from looking (in the words of one writer) like the horn of a rhinoceros to hanging like the trunk of an elephant (103).

Unlike the rooster or the ratite (ostriches, emus, and other flightless fowl), the male turkey stops at being a sire (Healy, 50). Though he is protective of his harem of hens during the mating season, he does not assist in locating a nest, protecting a brooding female, or raising his young. When the mating and nesting seasons are over, adult and juvenile male and female turkeys winter in sexually separate hierarchical flocks in the forest. In the spring, male and female come together on common ground, where they form harems consisting of a male and four, five, or six females. They court in a sequence of behaviors prompted mainly by the increasing daylight hours and to a lesser extent by warmer weather, which together activate the secretion of sex hormones that culminate in copulation (Healy, 47).

A hen signals her readiness to a displaying gobbler by separating herself from the other hens. She may do a kind of leaping dance around him and brush up against him before crouching in a manner that invites him to strut toward her and mount her from the rear. Treading and trampling her back with his feet and claws so as to cause her tail to rise, he lowers himself over her, their cloacae come into contact, sperm penetration takes place, and the mating is completed within four to five minutes from crouching to copulation (Healy, 50). The male thereupon gets down off the hen, who, like the chicken hen, straightens herself up and vigorously shakes out her body and feathers.

A single mating fertilizes a clutch of ten or more speckled eggs, which the hen takes the trouble to conceal in a shallow nest that she scrapes together with her beak in a wooded hideaway, preferably having both cover and undergrowth. She chooses a place that allows her to survey her surroundings as she sits on her eggs (Schorger, 255; Healy, 51) and to escape by rapid flight if necessary (Schorger, 257). The place she chooses is dry but close to water, and lies within a mile of the mating area. Laying an egg a day until the clutch size is reached, the female incubates her eggs continuously for twenty-six days after the last egg is laid, leaving the nest for ten to twenty minutes a day, as do chicken hens, to stretch, drink, defecate, and grab a bite, until the hatching gets underway. From then on, the female remains on the nest, fasting while the hatching takes place over a period of twenty-four-hours or so. Up to then, except for the daily excursions just mentioned, the brooding hen sits quietly, occasionally moving to turn her eggs and rearrange the dry leaves and twigs that constitute her nest, pecking from time to time at passing insects. She turns her eggs, generally more than once an hour, by raising her body slightly, sometimes standing all the way up, and reaching under her breast with her beak in response to cues from the embryos (Healy, 52).

The quality of life inside the egg is extremely important. According to Healy, "The social life of the turkey begins before it hatches and is well developed when it leaves the nest. At close range, pipping is audible, both the chipping sounds and a clicking vocalization. Hens respond to pipping sounds with soft clucking calls and with increased inspection and turning of eggs. Vocal communication between the hen and chicks in eggs synchronizes the hatching process and is critical to the survival of the chicks" (52–53).

The turkey hen's intelligence is evident in descriptions of those who have watched her secrete her nest in the (to us) wildest places, often in regions of the world that are completely new to her. Consider, for example, the hen who was transplanted from Ontario to Scotland, where she was confined for a while in a pen. Upon her release, she discovered and nested in a growth of ivy at the summit of a huge rock next to a tree. "Her mode of getting upstairs was original," an observer writes, "for she first of all got into the tree, and going along a branch that overhung the rock, let herself drop on to her nest; when on her nest not a vestige of her could be seen" (Quoted in Schorger, 257).

Joe Hutto says that turkeys have "an intricate aptitude, a clear distillation of purpose and design" (209), and that we need to rethink many of our "attitudes and presumptions about the complexity and profoundly subtle nature of the experience within other species" (199). His birds showed that they remembered places where they first met with foes such as a rattlesnake, as well as spots that delighted them. For example, whenever they got close to a creek they had previously enjoyed wading in and drinking from, they would "often run ahead, as if the place itself satisfied some need" (105).

Turkeys have home ranges and a strong sense of place, but they are not territorial in the sense of defending property as such (Healy, 48). Instead, they are what is known as pecking-order birds—birds, including chickens, turkeys, and quails, who recognize and respond to each other as individuals within their society (64). Chicks, turkey poults, and other precocial birds bond with their mothers from the earliest age before they are born, as we have seen. This bond, referred to as imprinting, on which the survival of the young depends, shows a capacity for complex memory formation and retention (Healy, 64). The chick, as Lesley Rogers explains in *Minds of Their Own,*

> learns the features of the hen and also of its siblings, and it remembers these for a very long time, possibly for the rest of its life. At first it forms a memory of the hen and follows her when she moves away from the nest. It also learns to recognize its siblings and can tell them apart from other chicks. Later it becomes sexually imprinted on the hen and this determines its preference for a mate in later life. It is these stable and powerful memories that direct its social behaviour. Chickens, when young and adult, must remember their positions in the social hierarchy (the pecking order) and to do this they must recognise other mem-

bers of their social group so that they can behave
appropriately when they encounter them. None of
these memories are simple. For example, the hen must
be recognised by her main visual features as well as her
vocalisations and the way she moves. Her smell may be
important also, as it is known that chicks imprint on
certain odours. The hen must be recognised in different environments (that is, she must be recognised
against a changing background of visual images,
sounds and smells). These memories are recorded in
the chick's brain and they must be, as it were, written
down according to some sort of chronological
sequence that becomes a unique autobiography of each
individual chick. (73–74)

Primatologists and others, says Rogers, are often too quick to
assume that only primates have complex social organizations and the
cognitive sophistication these organizations imply (1997, 74.)[4]
Meanwhile, turkeys, like chickens, have shown that they can recognize
and remember hundreds of individual flock members, and probably
more (Healy, 64), revealing a capacity for memory, social sophistication, and cognitive adaptability that is all the more remarkable when it
appears under highly stressful and unnatural conditions. It makes
sense, according to Rogers, that "for all mammalian and avian species,
the larger a social group is, the more complex the memories that each
individual must hold and the more often those memories have to be
updated. Overall, the memory abilities of [other] animals do not differ
from those of humans" (1997, 74).

Denigration of domesticated fowl is not warranted. In addition to
the unfairness of blaming the victim, too many factors can be mistak-
en for diminished cognitive capacity in these birds, from the masking
effects of the impoverished environments we force them to live in to

the complex infirmities we impose upon them that often include unrelieved pain whereby "extensive joint degeneration" (Duncan, *et al.*, 202; Danbury, *et al.*) and other physical disabilities, often occurring simultaneously, get confused with cognitive weakness. Moreover, people tend to see what they want to see. Those who impute simple-mindedness to animals, as Rogers says, are "expressing their attitudes to animals" rather than evidence or reason (Rogers, 1997, 75; Rogers and Kaplan, 169).

Especially when it comes to animals used for food, humanity's reasoning power and concern about fairness plummets. Witness the argument put forth by the Christian theologian John Cobb in his book, *Matters of Life and Death*. Concerning whether we have the right to cause extreme suffering to other species, Cobb places the life of human beings, nonhuman primates, and marine mammals above the life of chickens, veal calves, tuna, and sharks with respect to these species' capacity for personal experience, their value to "God" and to "others." While acknowledging that chickens, calves, tuna, and sharks value their own lives, Cobb maintains that "judgment" regards their feelings, their right to live, and their value to others as "not remarkably distinctive" (40). The world order and divine mind just happen to agree that animals humans like to eat, such as chickens, and animals who like to eat humans, such as sharks, have less valuable personal and interpersonal experiences and a lesser part in the universe. Ergo, it's okay for us to treat them worse.

Joe Hutto similarly mars his spiritual journey with gratuitous digs at domesticated fowl. Even the domesticated turkey's voice, he says at one point, is too "crude" for him and his wild turkey progeny to care about (235). When it comes to domesticated animals in this otherwise thoughtful book, the "spiritual union of the individual with the universe" doesn't apply (131). As an individual, the author is alienated from domesticated animals who, notwithstanding his contempt for them, are as much a part of the universe as their wild counterparts are

(Davis, 1990b). The "pen-raised poultry" Hutto despises derived from the "real wild turkeys" he adores (78). Whatever deficiencies they may have are the result of susceptibilities to human manipulation inherent in the turkey as such, whose resistance so far is even more impressive.

A related implication of Hutto's thought is that domesticated animals have forfeited and are not entitled to "spiritual union with the universe," a condition that automatically anathematizes the majority of humanity, which is a highly domesticated species. Thinking thus, Hutto links himself intentionally or unintentionally to the creatures he despises.

Illumination in the Flatwoods is a wonderful book, but it would have been more satisfying if the journey the author says stirred him to "rethink many of my attitudes and presumptions about the complexity and profoundly subtle nature of the experience within other species" (199) had included recognition of the fact that the experience of becoming "domesticated" is implicit within many, if not all, wild animals, including the turkey.

Several years ago, I published an essay called "Thinking Like a Chicken," a critique of environmental ethics (1995). In it, I noted how euphoric it feels to " 'think' like a Mountain"—or, in Hutto's case, a Wild Turkey. However, it does not feel good to think like the wild turkey's descendants and cousins on a factory farm or to put oneself vicariously through the events that put them there. It feels good to view oneself as an Environmental Hero in Chains seeking to unlock the key and run with the wild spirits of the earth. It does not feel good to see oneself through the eyes of one's quotidian victims. It is easier—and a lot more common, even among Great Souls—to blame the animal victims. Between those victims and the wild creatures they came from falls the shadow, the taboo. The anthropologist Edmund Leach calls such areas that it is not okay to explore, and of which it is not okay to speak honestly and truthfully, the "boundary percepts that lie between" the things society allows to be acknowledged (23). When television commentator Dan Rather once gushed over the Thanksgiving turkey that "there are memories in that bird," a voice from this shadowland of calculated invisibility said, yes, the turkey's memories of suffering, and you are eating them.

To suppress these voices, it may be rebutted that factory farmed turkeys do not have an emotional repertoire including a store of memories to worry about because domesticated animals are not really "animals" any more. Jeffrey Masson and Susan McCarthy address this argument in their book, *When Elephants Weep: The Emotional Lives of Animals*. They point out that the "emotions of captivity," whether the form of captivity be a body or a box, are as real as any other emotions (5–7).

Most of us have had the feeling at one time or other of being "locked up," "locked in," "bottled up," and "boxed in," but how many are prepared to say that such feelings are not real compared to the way we feel, say, taking a walk or watching a movie? Who is to say that an animal's memory of suffering is any less real because to us it is "silent" (Adams and Procter-Smith, 302)? To those who claim that captive animals are in "an unnatural situation," and therefore their feelings are not real or, if real, are not important, Masson and McCarthy reply,

> Humans are in just as unnatural a situation. We did not evolve in the world in which we now live either, with its deferred rewards and strange demands (sitting in classrooms or punching time clocks). All the same, we do not dismiss our emotions as not existing or inauthentic simply because they don't take place in small groups of hunter-gatherers on an African savanna, where human life is thought to have begun. We can be at a distance from our "origins" and still claim that our emotions are real and characteristic of our species. Why can't the same be true of [other] animals? It is not natural for

humans to be in prison. Yet if we are put in prison and
feel emotions that we don't usually feel, no one doubts
that they are real emotions. An animal in a zoo, or kept
as a pet, may feel emotions that it would not otherwise
have felt, but these are no less real. (6)

An emotional behavior in turkeys that Schorger says defies "logical
explanation" is "the great wake" the birds will hold over a fallen companion (150). In one episode he cites, the wing beats of a turkey hen
who had been shot "brought a flock that stopped beside the dying bird"
instead of running away as "expected" (149). Audubon reported how
after he had shot a turkey hen sitting on a fence, the males yelped in
answer to her cries as the wounded bird sat there. "I looked over the
log," he writes, "and saw about thirty fine cocks advancing rather cautiously towards the very spot where I lay concealed. They came so near
that the light in their eyes could easily be perceived, when I fired one
barrel, and killed three. The rest, instead of flying off, fell a strutting
around their dead companions" (quoted in Schorger, 149–150).

Similar behavior has been observed in domesticated turkeys on factory farms. When, as frequently happens in these places, a bird goes
into a convulsive heart attack, "[i]t is not uncommon to go into a bird
house and see the afflicted bird lying dead, surrounded by three or four
other birds that died because of the hysteria caused," according to a
poultry researcher (Kissell). This "hysteria" is not as the National
Turkey Federation would have us believe an example of the turkey's
lack of intelligence (Roberts, B8). On the contrary, it indicates a sensibility in these birds that should awaken us to how terribly we treat
them and make us stop it.

Others have marveled at "the great speed of the transplanting of
sound" from one bird to another within a flock at a moment's danger
and at "the pronounced degree of simultaneous and mutual beginning
and ending of 'bubbling' " of adult male turkeys in proximity to one

another. One bird having begun gobbling, the others follow him so quickly that "it is impossible for the human ear to detect an interval" or to determine which bird launched the chorus or caused it to cease (Schorger, 152).

Equally fascinating are the turkeys' frolics. In *Illumination in the Flatwoods*, Joe Hutto describes how on a morning in August his three-month-old turkeys, upon seeing him, drop from their roosting limbs where they had sat "softly chattering" in the dawn, "stretch their wings and do their strange little dance, a joyful, happy dance, expressing an exuberance" (154–155).

Not only do the young birds do this. A witness who chanced upon an evening dance of adult birds wrote:

> I heard a flock of wild turkeys calling....They were not calling strayed members of the flock. They were just having a twilight frolic before going to roost. They kept dashing at one another in mock anger, stridently calling all the while, almost playing leapfrog in their antics. Their notes were bold and clear....
>
> For about five minutes they played on the brown pine-straw floor of the forest, then as if at a signal, they assumed a sudden stealth and stole off in the glimmering shadows. (Quoted in Schorger, 153)

Another writer describes watching adult wild turkeys playing together on cold mornings:

> Frequently as many as eight or ten will participate in a sort of chase during which they will run at each other, then dodge suddenly, missing a collision by inches. Sometimes they will duck through or around a patch of

brush to put their companions off guard. (Quoted in
Schorger, 152)

In *The Minds of Birds*, Alexander Skutch devotes a lively chapter to
examples of such bird frolics, which he calls "fowl play." In his opinion,
"[o]f all our reasons for believing that birds are feeling creatures who
find satisfactions in their lives, their frolics are the most convincing"
(56).[5]

And consider birds' parental behavior. Skutch writes about the
behavior of birds who have lost their young. For hours or days, he says,
"I have watched bereaved parents continue to take food to nests deso-
lated by predation" (14). Persistence in bringing food for vanished
nestlings, which used to be regarded as a sign of avian stupidity, is now
more likely to be appreciated as a sign of parental emotional attach-
ment. In similar fashion, the bereaved parents in Robert Frost's poem,
"Home Burial," circle around the burial mound—the topic of the
death—of their infant son. Cows bellow—they cry—for days when
their newborn calves are taken away from them (Corea, 237; Clark,
299), and harp seal mothers have been photographed keeping watch
over the skinned bodies of their babies during a seal hunt (Davies). Far
from suggesting that these animals lack minds, feelings, and memories,
their behavior shows that they have them.

A turkey hen will fight fiercely to protect her young, showing how
her individual intelligence, ancestral memories, and maternal instincts
come together at just the right moment. An awed observer writes about
seeing a turkey hen spring into action to protect her young from a
hawk in rural Virginia, "[N]ow I have seen the turkey hen fight with a
passion that would make the eagle seem tame." In a published letter,
the person wrote:

I saw a turkey coming into the back field. She had
about 10 babies about the size of large quail walking

with her....Without warning, the hen took off vertical-
ly as if she had stepped on a mine. About 20 feet off the
ground, she intercepted and attacked a hawk that was
coming in for a baby. The hen hit the hawk with her
feet first and with [her] back almost parallel to the
ground. The hawk flew toward the back of the field
with the hen in pursuit; it turned back towards the
babies, and the hen hit it again. They both fell about 10
feet and were fighting with their feet, until the hawk
headed for the tree line and kept going. The hen
returned to her babies. When they went back into the
pines, the babies were very close to their mother's
feet....Wish you could have seen it. (Prosise)

In addition to flexible intelligence, turkeys, like humans, have a
fund of fixed behavior patterns, as do all animals. Behavior patterns
distinguish individuals and species from one another at the same time
that the possession of them links diverse forms of life together in a
common biological heritage. Behavior patterns confer identity while
providing a repertoire of responses that are ready to act: chicks instinctively seek cover in the presence of a moving overhead shadow, pregnant women discover they have an instinctual knowledge of how to be
mothers, children, similar to gallinaceous young birds, imprint on a
parent or parent substitute in infancy. Lacking a genetic inheritance of
behavior patterns, each individual would have to learn each new piece
of information anew, which would hasten the extinction of everyone.
Since every situation, regardless of how familiar and repetitive, contains
novelty, there is enough learning to do without the obvious disadvan-
tage of being a blank slate each time around.

But while many behavior patterns are blessings, others are not. We
can get stuck repeating what worked in one situation (say, an ancestor's
behavior or behavior that succeeded when we were ten) but doesn't in

this one, or we can get locked into a pattern of unreflecting assumptions, blind impulses, and false hopes. The Peanuts cartoon character Charlie Brown eternally succumbs to Lucy's football trick. This scene resonated so instinctively in everyone that it became an instant archetype in our culture. How can we, then, with our own susceptibility to irrational and nonrational repeat performances in the course of our lives, berate panicked turkeys for pacing wire fences to the point of being reduced to skin and bones, or for letting themselves get shot when reason and experience would say flee?

I opened this book with my introduction to turkeys a number of years ago. I would like to close this chapter with my memory of Priscilla and Mila, two white turkey hens who lived with my husband and me for several years until they died. Victims of a truck accident, they both would have been dead by the time we adopted them if they had not been rescued. Though roughly the same age, these two hens were very different from each other. Mila was a gentle and pacific turkey with an intent, watchful face. Priscilla was a moody hen with emotional burdens. Throughout the spring and summer Priscilla would disappear into the woods around our house and I would have to go look for her. Eventually I would spy her white form nestled in thick vegetation, where she laid many clutches of eggs that, since there was no male turkey to fertilize them, would never hatch. Priscilla kept trying to be a mother, and doubtless in part because she could not realize her desire to be one, she was out of temper much of the time.

When Priscilla got into one of her bad moods, you could see her getting ready to charge my husband or me, and maybe bite us, which wasn't pleasant. With her head pulsing colors and her yelps sounding a warning, she glared at us with combat in her whole demeanor. What stopped her was Mila. Perking up her head at the signals, Mila would enter directly into the path between Priscilla and us, and block her. She would tread back and forth in front of Priscilla, uttering soft pleading yelps as if beseeching her not to charge. Priscilla would gradually calm down.

I do not know whether what I saw taking place between Mila and
Priscilla has any connection to Konrad Lorenz's description of what happens when two male turkeys have been fighting and one of them wants
to quit. According to Lorenz, the one who has had enough makes a
"specific submissive gesture which serves to forestall the intent of the
attack" (194). He lies down with his neck stretched out on the ground.
At this, "the victor behaves exactly as a wolf or dog in the same situation, that is to say, he evidently wants to peck and kick at the prostrated enemy, but simply cannot: he would if he could but he can't! So, still
in threatening attitude, he walks round and round his prostrated rival,
making tentative passes at him, but leaving him untouched" (194).

In the case of Mila and Priscilla, the belligerent hen submitted to
the peacemaker's inhibiting signals. Information was communicated,
learned, used, and remembered by both hens in what must have been
for them a genetically familiar, yet novel, situation. It involved two
female birds derived from a background of genetic selection for "meat-
type" characteristics supposedly linked to a reduction in brain weight
or size—crude measures of intelligence in an era dominated by the
knowledge and armed with the power of subatomic particles, genes,
and nanotechnology.

Some scientists now speculate that the "special ability of the avian
brain to make new neurons in adulthood" may go far to explain why
birds, despite "their comparatively small brains," can perform such
incredibly sophisticated cognitive feats as they are now known to
accomplish (Rogers, 1995, 217). According to Rogers, "There has been
a tradition of treating birds as cognitively inferior to mammalian
species as they have smaller brain to body weight ratios and they lack
the neocortex,...but recent behavioural research is challenging this concept....Recent findings challenge assumptions that have been made

about brain size and the superiority of the mammalian line of evolution" (1995, 214).

The point is not to pit mammals and birds against each other in
terms of IQ, any more than the pitting of wild and domestic animals
against each other, humans against nonhuman animals, or one human
society against another is the best way to increase our knowledge and better our relationships with those we are trying to understand. Joe Hutto
says in his book about the wild turkeys he raised and loved, "Whether
attempting to achieve understanding of an exotic culture or an unfamil-
iar species, a position of superiority is always a recipe for failure"(4).

Is this observation any less true in trying to understand a familiar
culture or a familiar species? Regarding things close at hand, it could be
an even harder proposition to live by, while upholding the necessity of
judgment in regard to any culture, familiar or foreign, that some things
are better or worse than others, or simply right or wrong. The idea that
human slavery is wrong has gained such unquestioning acceptance in
Western society as to have assumed the status of a fact. Yet, in reality,
this is a moral principle which is based on a selection of facts that,
through centuries of social struggle and intellectual debate, have come
to be regarded as preeminent over other facts that have led or could
lead to different conclusions about slavery.

Some philosophers have argued that values cannot logically derive
from facts. Peter Singer writes for example that "[s]ome versions of
Social Darwinism commit the fallacy of deducing values from facts,"
but "the gap between facts and values remains as unbridgeable as it was
when David Hume first drew attention to it in 1739" (1999, 12).
However, this is disputable. Sentience is a fact from which values have
logically derived and in the viewpoint of many *should* derive. Isn't this
what Jeremy Bentham meant when he said in support of animals'
rights, the question is not whether animals can reason, but whether
they suffer? Is empathy not vested in the sensible difference we perceive
between a sufferer and a stone? In *Factory Farming*, Andrew Johnson

asserts the connection between fact and value in pointing out the falla-cy in the argument that "cruelty to other species is wrong solely as a bad example which may encourage cruelty to humans" (104). For, he says, "[i]f it really had no other significance, it could not possibly be a bad example. No-one would claim that the mineralogist who enjoys slicing sections of rock to display the pretty colours within should be regard-ed as a danger to society, who might soon turn to slicing up human beings. No objection to cruelty can hold water, if it is not accompanied by an objection to the resultant suffering on its own moral account" (104–105).

That values can derive from facts can be seen in many other ways as well. Amid the many considerations that constitute eating, for instance, the facts that affect one most powerfully determine one's dietary choices and values, which derive therefrom. If, for example, the fact that one's meat-eating family wants its members to eat traditional-ly is more compelling to one than the knowledge of what an animal must endure in order to become a meal, one will eat traditionally, in the presence of the family at least, accordingly. The question is, how can an anonymous animal and that animal's situation be made to stand out for the majority of people as a matter of overriding fact and thus as a basis of fundamental principle amid the competing forces of culture and other considerations that get in the way?

1. Jukes's father, chemist Thomas Jukes, promoted the use of antibiotics as growth promot-ers in farmed animals. In 1949, he identified tetracycline dumped by the pharmaceutical company American Cyanamid into the Pearl River in New York City as the cause of over-large fish. In laboratory experiments that followed, "Chicks grew 10 to 20 percent faster than those on plain rations. Piglets did even better" (Brownlee).

2. For critiques of the personhood criteria of The Great Ape Project, see Rogers 1997, *Minds of Their Own*, 190–194; Bekoff 1998; Davis, 1995–1996; Davis 2001c; Davis 2001d.

3. When, in 1999, People for the Ethical Treatment of Animals published two undercover investigations, one showing intense cruelty to pregnant sows on a pig breeding farm in North Carolina, the other showing intense cruelty to young turkeys on a Minnesota

turkey farm, media covered the pig cruelty case, which resulted in felony indictments, but showed no similar interest in the turkey-farm exposé, which included video of a farm manager culling sick, lame, and injured birds by wringing their necks, bludgeoning them with a metal pipe and pliers, and throwing the beaten, still-living birds into dead piles. Prosecution efforts failed (PETA). Yet, when a Minnesota state trooper intentionally ran his squad car over a turkey hen popular with townspeople in a Minneapolis suburb on May 3, 2001, he was immediately charged with cruelty to animals and people were outraged, though the case was dropped on May 31 (State of MN). *Minneapolis Star Tribune* reporter Terry Collins told me on May 22 in a phone conversation that the amount of public distress on behalf of this particular turkey "was unexpected." (See Collins)

4.   See also biologist Marc Bekoff's argument for avoiding "[n]arrow-minded primatocentrism and specisism" in "studies of animal cognition and animal protection and rights" (269).

5.   Consider the ostrich's ballet: "Especially in the early morning, a few birds in a group will suddenly receive a mystic, inaudible cue and begin to dance in circles on tip-toes, with outstretched wings. Very soon the whole group will join spontaneously in the twirling dance [which] may be a primeval urge or merely an expression of the joy of being alive" (Holtzhausen and Kotze, 52, 54).

9

INVENTING NEW TRADITIONS

If biting into a turkey drumstick on Thanksgiving isn't covered by "life, liberty and the pursuit of happiness," then what is?
—Richard Berman, "Patrolling your private life"

We do not see our own personal meat eating as contact with animals because it has been renamed as contact with food.
—Carol J. Adams and Marjorie Procter-Smith, 298

The question before us is, which images of the universe, of power, of animals, of ourselves, will we represent in our food?
—Carol J. Adams, *The Sexual Politics of Meat*, 202

Cattle, sheep, swine, asses, mules, and goats, along with chickens, geese, and turkeys, all agreed enthusiastically to give their names back to the people to whom—as they put it—they belonged.—Ursula Le Guin, "She Unnames Them"

CELEBRATION CAN INCLUDE EVOLUTION. JUST AS Western culture long ago substituted bread and wine for animal (and human) sacrifice in traditional religious celebrations, as in the Christian Eucharist, which is literally a "Thanksgiving" (Visser, *Rituals*, 36), so the tofu turkey and many other nonanimal food choices are replacing the traditional corpse at the festive meal in a growing number of households (Hagenbaugh). Few people are clamoring for a return to the days of bloody altars and struggling victims in places of worship or in home and restaurant kitchens. If such sights are no longer acceptable to the majority of Western society, how can they continue to be justified behind the scenes?

Yet even today, what is done to animals for food takes place throughout much of the world out in the open, with little or no protest—the opposite, in fact. Either the ritual of animal food production is so visible a part of the culture or subculture as to render the animals invisible to those who see and engage in it day in and day out, or else it takes place hidden inside a factory farm and a "processing plant," and the animals are rendered invisible that way.

This is a dilemma that animals used for food, and ultimately all animals, face. It isn't only in the future being fashioned by genetic engineering that turkeys and chickens and cows and pigs will have no more real life than a light bulb in the eyes of most people. Nor is it only in the Western world that these animals suffer and die "unseen." In just about any traditional country in the world, animals are treated openly with great cruelty and indifference in the food markets, where their cries ring out unheeded among the fruits and vegetables, the haggling and merchandise. Then again, in the southeastern United States, you see people buying and consuming chickens in the supermarkets and restaurants as the birds are being trucked up and down the roads to the slaughterhouses, and even falling out of trucks in the middle of town right in front of their eyes. Local produce markets dot the highways of the Eastern Shore and right behind them sit three or four long, low houses with sixty thousand to eighty thousand or more invisible birds inside.

A woman who worked for a turkey company in England said of the birds that, from the time they are born until they are slaughtered at three months old or so, "[t]hey all live in hell, all the time that they are alive. And no one cares" (Hall, 1984, 84). At the slaughterhouse, when the coffee break sirens sounded, the kill crew dropped everything and left the turkeys hanging upside down from the conveyer belts until they came back from their break to electrocute and kill them (83).

Alice Munro's story "The Turkey Season," which is set in a turkey slaughterhouse in a rural town in Ontario, Canada during the pre-Christmas season, is remarkable for the fact that it does not have any live turkeys or slaughter scenes in it. The narrator, recalling her experience as a turkey gutter when she was fourteen, says, "All I could see when I closed my eyes, the first few nights after working there, was turkeys. I saw them hanging upside down, plucked and stiffened, pale and cold, with the heads and necks limp, the eyes and nostrils clotted with dark blood....I saw them not with aversion but with a sense of endless work to be done" (61). The story could have been set almost anywhere.

Today, in the United States, it is not unusual for two or three turkeys to be placed in a pen outside small slaughtering operations during the holidays to encourage people to purchase freshly slaughtered birds inside or else choose the bird they wish to have killed for themselves while they wait. Our turkeys Boris and Florence came from the Potomac Poultry Company in Baltimore, Maryland, where they were used to attract customers prior to their release to our sanctuary, thanks to two Baltimore residents, Terry Kleeman and Marie Gleason. Recalling his childhood in England, animal rights theologian Andrew Linzey recalls how the butcher shops "used to hang dead turkeys outside their stores at Christmas" to attract customers. Linzey is unusual, and perhaps unique, among Christian thinkers and perhaps the whole world for stating that his initial revelation of the connection between meat and the death of a living creature took place when he was four or five years old, when his mother "placed a large turkey on the Christmas table" (1998).

Regarding Christianity, Linzey argues that the central event of the incarnation is "not just God's 'yes' to one person living in first-century Palestine, or to humans as a species, but to all flesh, both human and animal" (1998). Could the Christian religion ever come to the point of respecting "all flesh," not in false ceremonies of compassion, but in fact? Does Christianity have the capacity to extend the symbolism implicit in the image of animals present at the birth of Christ to incorporate inclusion of all creatures within the realm of the Golden Rule? Linzey points out that Christianity's archetypal nativity scene does not even appear in the canonical New Testament gospels of Matthew, Mark, Luke, and John. Like the bits and pieces of traditions in general, it was put into place later, in the case of the animals around the baby Jesus, centuries later. At the same time, it harks back to the Orphic tradition of animals being drawn to a pacific embodiment of humanity.

Are such images doomed to being, as the American writer, Henry Miller, said of Thoreau and Walden, and could have said about St. Francis and the Birds, primarily symbols and tokens of a reality we do not really want except as a tease, and not so much from a desire to protect the ideal from pollution by the real, but to protect the real from being "spoiled" by the ideal? Ironically, in the case of animal rights, it is the "idealists" who keep trying to focus society's attention on lives and individuals, the realm in which "Life" manifests itself, versus those who intone formalistically about Life and Species and invoke platitudes of Apology to and Respect for the Animal, while treating actual animals in ways that are little or no different from the ways of those who profess no respect for the Environment or the Animal at all.

Just as the environmental movement has largely excluded individual nonhuman creatures from its purview, making it, as philosopher Michael Allen Fox writes, "ethically myopic and no more than self-serving" (1993, 122), so the Reverend Andrew Linzey observes, "there is something distinctly odd, even perverse, about an incarnational spirituality that cannot celebrate our relations with other creatures" (1999, 15). Theologians, he says, who are "eager, sometimes over-eager, to see incarnational resonances within almost every area of human activity (art, music, poetry, dance)...look with astonishment at the idea that our relations with animals might be an issue worthy of spiritual, nay incarnational, concern" (1999, 15).

In his essay "Against Zoos," philosopher Dale Jamieson offers a look at how we value and do not value creatures who are not human. He raises the question of whether, for example, confining a few Mountain Gorillas in a zoo rather than allowing the species to die out—preserving species at all costs with scant or no regard for the life and experience of the remnant individuals—doesn't amount to a sacrifice of "the lower-case gorilla for the upper-case Gorilla" (115). In the past, gorillas didn't count as individuals in their own right, which is why they have virtually ceased to exist, and now under a new guise, they still don't count. As Jamieson says, their genes matter more than they do (115).

As for the wild turkey, brought back from the edge of extinction because when it comes to killing only the lower-case bird can satisfy, "[t]he object is to go into the woods with whatever gun and load you have that offers the absolute best odds for an instant, clean kill. The majestic wild turkey certainly deserves no less" (Brister, 1348).

Being "majestic" and "sacred" has not saved animals. On the contrary, trophy hunting (isn't all sport hunting trophy hunting?) and the cruel sacrifice of animals in the name of religion throughout history and in many places throughout the world today show what traditional concepts of sanctification and majesty have meant for animals. Recall that being "sacred" for a turkey in Pueblo societies meant ritual strangulation, live burial, and other cruelties—cruelties that, if the turkey's point of view counts, make the Pueblos' motivations irrelevant. The writer Heather Mac Donald asks how the idea of Native Americans "living in balance" with nature accords with their running the buffalo off cliffs. Did the buffalo, too, "feel in perfect harmony with nature?" (127). And why, she asks, are African-American voodoo rituals more "harmonious" than cultivating livestock? (131) A *National Geographic* article on "The African Roots of Voodoo" suggests an answer

(Beckwith and Fisher, 109). The fact that Mac Donald does not cast an equally critical eye on the white America of a "glorious revolutionary past" (131), and may not care about animals, or humans for that matter, does not invalidate these questions.

People look to the mythic past for prototypes in order to propagate some plan or hope for the present and future, to protect existing traditions and outlooks, or to advance new practices and prospects from the vital elements within these myths that have yet to be exploited. This is the true use of the Golden Age and the Garden of Eden and other myths of origin, including America's national origin myth of Thanksgiving. These myths act as informing principles of existence, and in this sense they can promote ethical insight and change, or they can be invoked ironically to protect the "fallen world" from their infiltration, which is how they have mainly been used with respect to how we view and treat the other members of the animal kingdom to which we belong.

How a myth of origin will be used is primarily a matter of will, because people change their traditions all the time on the basis of allegiances they otherwise cling to. Customs come and go. Historian Jackson Lears has pointed out how many "time-honored traditions" of today were "created overnight." Saluting the flag, singing Christmas carols, exchanging engagement rings and wedding vows—these are a few of the "sacred" things he mentions. In his view, recognizing that people invent traditions to meet new and changing needs can be liberating because it allows us to feel freer to revise our traditions to meet our own changing needs and evolving perceptions, for example to eat "vegetarian chili instead of roast beef or goose for Christmas dinner."

All of which, Lears says, is in keeping with "the good American tradition of starting over, reinventing the self." Thus a New Yorker tells the *Washington Post* that she and other Americans too busy to cook are "thankful for turkey takeout" at Thanksgiving: "The Norman Rockwell picture doesn't exist anymore....But you can re-create it if you order it"

(Walsh). Notice this New Yorker isn't suggesting that takeout is an inferior substitute for doing your own cooking in her opinion, any more than conservative Americans have been known to complain that the Norman Rockwell picture of Thanksgiving is an inferior substitute for the "real" Thanksgiving because no Native Americans are in the picture.

The American Thanksgiving, which is rooted in ancient harvest festival traditions to which it bears some resemblance (Love; Sickel) has been "recreated" many times over; fabricated, as James W. Loewen shows in his chapter, "The Truth about the First Thanksgiving" (95); and metamorphosed like mad, as Elizabeth Pleck shows in *Celebrating the Family*. Arguably, vegetarians who spend hours preparing a tofu turkey or a chestnut casserole from scratch in their kitchens express the spirit of Thanksgiving more authentically than the turkey takeout people do, while taking the American tradition of the pioneer to a new level of adventure and nurture.

Substitution of new materials for previously used ones to celebrate a tradition is an integral part of tradition. In the religious realm, if we can substitute animal flesh for human flesh and bread and wine for "all flesh" and the shedding of innocent blood, and view these changes as advances of civilization and not as inferior substitutes for genuine religious experience, we are ready to go forward in our everyday lives on ground that is already laid. If God can become flesh, then flesh can become fruit. Technologically, this transformation, this substitution, has already occurred because people have demanded it and technology can meet that demand (Schlosser). If the Peaceable Kingdom is a genuine desire and a practicable prospect, fake meat is the food to which dead meat has aspired, and the fake meat makers are as deserving as anyone is of the Nobel Prize for Peace.

"In the past," says the author of the book *The Evolving Self and Creativity*, "our limbic system learned to produce...disgust at the smell of rotten meat. Now we might be learning to experience disgust at the thought of eating meat in the first place——thanks to values that are the result of consciousness" (Csikszentmihalyi).

This book has looked at the role of the Thanksgiving turkey in American culture. It has attempted to separate the caricature of the Native American bird from the bird divested of that baggage and image as a being in its own right. At the same time it has formulated its own construct of the turkey as a sentinel animal. The cultural turkey in America is a model figure that allows us to examine our attitudes and the values they imply, like the values implicit in creating laughingstocks and innocent victims in order to be thankful, and the values of a nation that ritually constitutes itself by consuming an animal—one, moreover, that it despises and mocks as part of a patriotic celebration proclaiming the wholesome virtues of family life.

The turkey is "more than a meal" in the sense that every creature is more than a meal outside the range of those who prey on it. The turkey is more than a meal at Thanksgiving, just as the Thanksgiving ritual is more than "merely a midday dinner consisting of a particular bird" surrounded by TV football, family reunions, cranberry sauce, and sweet potatoes (Copeland, C1). But is it a cultural expression of values that are the result of consciousness?

I have sought to draw attention to the moral ecology surrounding the Thanksgiving turkey, the miasma around the traditional holiday meal. The ritual taunting of the sacrificial bird that is conducted by the media each year—what if this mean-spirited foreplay and blood sacrifice were taken away? What elements of Thanksgiving remain? Hunters have claimed that the killing they do is incidental to their joy of being in the woods, and turkey eaters have claimed that the carnage they inflict is incidental to their appetite for togetherness (Goodman). Yet the carnage both inflict is the one thing in the midst of other changes on which these people stand firm, as if Plymouth Rock amounted in the final analysis to little more than a pile of meat, as the symbol of happiness does in the final epiphany of Scrooge.

Slowly, this pile may be rotting away. As the new millennium unfolds in America, the conflict between the vegetarians and the meat-eaters, animal rights people, and the rest of society, appears most clearly at Thanksgiving. As the single most visible animal symbol in America, the de facto symbol of the nation and the "icon of American food" (Berman, 1998, A19), the turkey brings into focus this conflict and marks its progress in a holiday in which personal values and cultural ideals come together most notably.

In December 2000, a recall of 16.7 million pounds of turkey meat contaminated with the bacterial pathogen *Listeria monocytogenes* (AP) prompted vegetarian health advocates to warn that "[a]s long as Americans make meat the center of our cholesterol-laden culinary tradition and consume no fewer than one million animals per hour, foodborne illness will remain a fact of life" (Barnard).[1] In contrast, an attractive feature of pasta, potatoes, and other plant foods "is that they have no intestines where virulent bacteria may incubate" (Barnard). So far, the standard media response has been to dismiss these "grim health warnings" (Eisner) and vegetarian alternatives (Fox, 1998, 378–79; Schlosser, 2001b, 257), just as the specter of animal suffering and animal rights is reviled for "emasculat[ing] our beloved family recipes," cooling "warm memories of feasts gone by," and threatening such feasts in the future (Berman, 1998). But the scoffers who invoke these messages only to scorn them do not inevitably deny them and may even be said to be warming up to their validity as part of an overall trend (Hanks; Kaye).

Thus far, the vegetarian animal rights message appears mainly in media contexts reflecting a culture shaping process that has aptly been called "dominance through mentioning" (Loewen, 85–86). In dominance through mentioning, disturbing truths and iconoclastic viewpoints are "mentioned" so that the opinion makers cannot be accused of omitting them, and to spice up otherwise dull fare—"a beak in the monotony," so to speak (Jones, 1996, B2). But they are inserted in a rhetoric intended to diminish their significance and influence. In *Lies My Teacher Told Me*, sociologist James Loewen points out that few of his college students can ever recall the European plague that destroyed the Wampanoag town of Patuxet (and scores of other Native American towns and villages), a devastation that enabled the Pilgrims to take over the town and rename it Plymouth, because American textbook writers have traditionally buried the plague (if they even mentioned it) in a few bland phrases surrounded by glorification of the Pilgrims and the Plymouth Harbor scenery.

Similarly, the cruelty of turkey production and positive views of turkeys appear in an overriding media context that makes light and fun of both the suffering and intelligence of these birds. More than anything else, as Loewen observes, it is the attitude toward the information presented that constitutes the "dominance" that ensures that society's collective amnesia and willful forgetting will remain intact at Thanksgiving, ironically the holiday when memories are supposed to be in the ascendant.

At the present time, an analysis of media trends concerning animal rights and vegetarianism at Thanksgiving during the past fifty years would be worth undertaking. We've come a long way since the days when a lone voice in the *New York Times* urged that the Presidential turkey should be put in a "humane coma" prior to being killed, and columnists Jack Anderson and Joseph Spear published what at the time was an unusual Thanksgiving commentary about the threat of human illnesses as a result of eating turkeys and other animals raised for food and the growing inability of antibiotics to treat these illnesses. Such messages are now a part of Thanksgiving, and have become more challenging and insistent than ever before.

Thanksgiving 2000 saw the range of media attitudes towards turkeys and vegetarianism that have come into being over the past few decades. Film critic Richard Roeper's commentary on celebrity film star Alicia Silverstone's "Dear Friends" letter, from which he quoted generous excerpts, is a touchstone for values that are currently in flux in America concerning animal rights and vegetarianism, as well as the meaning and means of celebration. Roeper says he perked up when he saw Alicia's name sparkling among his email clutter during the holiday. His roguish remarks surrounding "Silverstone's bold stand for the rights of turkeys," while anything but radical, are not unreceptive to her message, the essence of which he gives as follows.

> Dear Friends:
>
> It's that time of year again when we gather with friends and family to celebrate and give thanks for all the good fortune we have in our lives. Thanksgiving is such a meaningful holiday that is, unfortunately, tainted by the slaughter of helpless turkeys.
>
> Thanksgiving should be a celebration of life....So, it doesn't make sense to celebrate that with a dead bird in the middle of the table....
>
> The good news is that there are natural, healthier alternatives that have become wildly popular and taste so good you won't miss turkey a bit....
>
> We all have our ways of celebrating the holidays, and I certainly don't want to force mine on anyone. But if you've ever wondered whether there was a more humane way to celebrate, I want you to know there is.

Roeper responds in this vein. Okay, Alicia, I'm game, as long as you don't mind if I wash down "a more humane way to celebrate" with wine that was made from the carcasses of dead grapes.

To which, at this stage of our life, it may simply be said of such wine, it's better than blood.

1. "Food-borne diseases in America cause an estimated 76 million illnesses annually, resulting in 325,000 hospitalizations and about 5,000 deaths, according to a new study by the CDC [Centers for Disease Control]. It is an epidemic that costs upwards of $30 billion in medical expenses and lost productivity, by government estimates" (Perl, 2000, 11).

References and Bibliography ⌁

Articles mentioning, featuring, or highlighting United Poultry Concerns are starred. All A.W. Schorger citations with the exception of a reference to a 1961 article noted in the text are to his book *The Wild Turkey: Its History and Domestication* published in 1966.

Adams, Carol J., and Marjorie Procter-Smith. 1993."Taking Life or 'Taking on Life': Table Talk and Animals." In *Ecofeminism and the Sacred*, ed. Carol J. Adams, 295–310. New York: Continuum.

Adams, Carol J. 1995a. *Neither Man nor Beast: Feminism and the Defense of Animals*. New York: Continuum.

_____. 1995b. "Bestiality: the unmentioned abuse." *Animals' Agenda* 15.6 (November-December): 29–31.

_____. 2000. *The Sexual Politics of Meat: A Feminist-Vegetarian Critical Theory*. New York: Continuum. First published, 1990.

Ambler, R. W. 1975. "The Transformation of Harvest Celebrations in Nineteenth-Century Lincolnshire." *Midland History* 3.1: 298–306.

Anderson, Jack, and Joseph Spear. 1987. "What's Wrong With Thanksgiving Dinner." *Washington Post* 26 November: G9.

AP (Associated Press). 1947. "Truman's Yule Turkey is 47-Pound Champion." *New York Times* 16 December: 46.

_____. 1953. "A 39-Pound Turkey Is Presented to the Eisenhowers." *New York Times* 17 November: 32.

_____. 1955. "Destined for President's Table." *New York Times* 15 November: 20.

_____. 1963. "Kennedy Spares the Life of 55-Pound Gift Turkey." *New York Times* 20 November: 34.

_____. 1977. "White House Turkey Accepted by Mondale." *New York Times* 16 November: A15.

_____. 1994. "Turkeys Are Also For Bowling." 24 November.

_____. 1997. "Lucky bird gets presidential pardon." *Democrat and Chronicle* 24 November: 14A.

_____. 1998. "Turkey has president to thank for its life." *Virginian-Pilot* 25 November: A3.

_____. 2000. "Deaths, miscarriages linked to recalled turkey." 15 December.

Atwood, Margaret. 1989. *Cat's Eye.* New York: Doubleday. 138–139.

Bakeless, John. 1961. *America As Seen By Its First Explorers: The Eyes of Discovery.* New York: Dover. First published as *The Eyes of Discovery* 1950.

Bakhtin, Mikhail. 1967. *Rabelais and His World.* Trans. Helene Iswolsky. Cambridge: MIT Press.

Bakst, M.R., and G.J. Wishart, eds. 1995. *Proceedings: First International Symposium on the Artificial Insemination of Poultry.* Savoy, Il: The Poultry Science Association.

Baldino, Paul. 1997. Letter to author, 18 November.

Balian, Lorna. 1973. *Sometimes It's Turkey—Sometimes It's Feathers.* Nashville, TN: Abingdon Press.

Barber, Theodore Xenophon. 1993. *The Human Nature of Birds: A Scientific Discovery with Startling Implications.* New York: St. Martin's Press.

Barnard, Neal H. 2000. "Cutting back on meat, poultry reduces bacteria threats." *Virginian-Pilot* 29 December: Hampton Roads.

Bartlett, Kim. 1998. "Riding the Wave Length: A Discussion on Interspecies Communication with Jim Nollman." *Animals' Agenda* (June): 6–10.

Bauman, Batya. 1998. "Turkey Sacrifice." Email to Chickadee-1@envirolink.org, 30 November.

Bedard, Paul. 1991. "Bush saves turkeys' necks, not his own." *Washington Times* 27 November: A1, A9.

Beirne, Piers. 1997. "Rethinking Bestiality: Towards a Concept of Interspecies Sexual Assault." *Theoretical Criminology* 1.3: 317–340.

Bekoff, Marc. 1998. "Deep Ethology, Animal Rights, and the Great Ape/Animal Project: Resisting Speciesism and Expanding the Community of Equals." *Journal of Agricultural and Environmental Ethics* 10: 269–296.

Benet, Sula, ed. 1990. "Holidays and Holy Days." *The Encyclopedia Americana.* Vol. 14.

_____. "Thanksgiving Day." Vol. 26.

Benjamin, Earl W., and Howard C. Pierce. 1937. *Marketing Poultry Products.* New York: John Wiley & Sons.

Bentham, Jeremy. 1970. *An Introduction to the Principles of Morals and Legislation.* Introd. Laurence J. LaFleur. Darien, CT: Hafner Publishing Co. Chapter 17, 310–311 footnote.

Bettelheim, Bruno. 1980. *Surviving and Other Essays.* New York: Vintage Books.

Berger, John. 1985. "Why Look at Animals?" In *The Language of the Birds: Tales, Texts, & Poems of Interspecies Communication,* ed. David M. Guss, 275–287. San Francisco: North Point Press.

Berman, Richard. 1997. "Patrolling your private life." *Washington Times* 27 November: A18.

_____. 1998. "Turkey police, beware." *Washington Times* 26 November: A19.

Bigelow, John, ed. 1904. *The Works of Benjamin Franklin in Twelve Volumes*. Federal Edition. Vol. 10. New York: Knickerbocker Press-G.P. Putnam's Sons.

*Cacchioli, Joseph. 1999. "For love of the birds." *Daily Times* (Salisbury, MD) 28 November: B1–B2.

Bird Brain. 1999. *People* 13 December: 188.

Bliss, William Root. 1893. "A Thanksgiving." *The Old Colony Town and the Ambit of Buzzards Bay*. Boston and New York: Houghton, Mifflin and Co.

Blosser, John, and James McCandlish. 1989. "It's Sick! Yellville Turkeys Tossed Out of Planes—For Fun." *National Enquirer* 5 December.

*Bock, James. 1992. "We Gather Together." *Sun* (Baltimore) 26 November: 1A, 15A.

Borenstein, Seth. 1998. Knight Ridder. "Turkey lovers rejoice as wild bird population rebounds." *Albuquerque Journal* 26 November: B5.

*Borgman, Anna. 1994. "Turkey's for the Birds, Vegetarian Diners Say." *Washington Post* 25 November: C1.

*_____. 1996. "Protesters Say No Thanks to Turkey Dinner." *Washington Post* 27 November: D5.

Bradford, William. 1981. *Of Plymouth Plantation 1620–1647*. Introd. Francis Murphy. New York: Modern Library. First printed in entirety 1856.

Brandenberger, Joel. Lobbyist, National Turkey Federation. 1998. Email to David J. Cantor, 23 October.

Brister, Bob. 1975. "Tighten Up for Turkey." *Field & Stream* 79 (April): 1344–1348.

Brody, Jane E. 1997. "Wild Turkeys Return to American Fields." *New York Times* 25 November: C1, C6.

Brownlee, Shannon. 2000. "What We Really Pay For Cheap Meat." *Washington Post* 21 May: B3.

Brush, Stephanie. 1989. "When Fur Starts to Fly." *Washington Post* 13 August: B1, F8.

Bubbly-jock. 1989. *Oxford English Dictionary*, 2nd ed. Vol. 2.

_____. 1941. *Scottish National Dictionary*. Vol. 2.

Burkert, Walter, *et al.* 1987. *Violent Origins: Ritual Killing and Cultural Formation*, ed. Robert G. Hamerton-Kelly. Stanford: Stanford UP.

Caras, Roger A. 1996. *A Perfect Harmony: The Intertwining Lives of Animals and Humans Throughout History*. New York: Simon & Schuster.

Carlson, Peter. 1999. "Let Us Give Pranks: The Holiday's Irreverent Past." *Washington Post* 25 November: C1, C10.

Cartmill, Matt. 1993. *A View to a Death in the Morning: Hunting and Nature through History*. Cambridge: Harvard UP.

*Carton, Barbara. 1996. "Mommy, Why Did Auntie Put Birdie Inside the Oven?" *Wall Street Journal* 26 November: A1, A10.

Cavalieri, Paola, and Peter Singer. 1993. *The Great Ape Project: Equality beyond Humanity*. New York: St. Martin's Press.

Chapman, Frank M. 1933. *Autobiography of a Bird-Lover.* New York and London: D. Appleton-Century Co.

Christman, Carolyn J., and Robert O. Hawes. 1999. *Birds of a Feather: Saving Rare Turkeys From Extinction.* Pittsboro, NC: American Livestock Breeds Conservancy.

Clark, Walter Van Tilburg. 1975. "The Indian Well." In *The Western Story: Fact, Fiction, and Myth,* ed. Philip Durham and Everett L. Jones, 290–303. New York: Harcourt Brace Jovanovich.

Clinton, Bill. 1997. "Remarks By the President At National Turkey Pardoning Ceremony." Washington, D.C.: The White House Office of the Press Secretary, 26 November.

Cobb, John B, Jr. 1992. *Matters of Life and Death.* Louisville, KY: Westminster/John Knox Press.

Collins, Terry. 2001. "Trooper received mixed direction on handling Chaska turkey." *Star Tribune* 11 May: Metro.

Colton, Michael. 1997. "Fowl-Weather Friend: President Clinton Saves the Life of Willis, a Turkey for Our Times." *Washington Post* 27 November: D1, D13.

Cominou, Maria. 1995. "Speech, Pornography, and Hunting." In *Animals and Women: Feminist Theoretical Explorations,* ed. Carol J. Adams and Josephine Donovan, 126–148. Durham and London: Duke UP.

Conaway, James. 1992. "Eastern Wildlife—Bittersweet Success: Wild turkey." *National Geographic* 181.2: 74–77.

Contreras, Patricia. 1983. "Wild Turkey: A Real All-American Bird." *New York Times* 20 November, Sec. 11: 27.

Cook, Christopher D. 1999. "Fowl Trouble." *Harper's Magazine* (August): 78–79.

Copeland, Libby Ingrid. 1998. "A Flight To the Feast Of Family." *Washington Post* 26 November: C1, C16.

Corea, Gena. 1985. *The Mother Machine: Reproductive Technologies from Artificial Insemination to Artificial Wombs.* New York: Harper & Row.

Csikszentmihalyi, Mihaly. 1999. "It's All in Your Head." *Washington Post Book World* 16 May: 3.

Cuny, Lynn. 1996. "Miles and Priscilla (November): n.p." *Newsletter.* Boerne, TX: Wildlife Rescue & Rehabilitation, Inc.

Curcio, Barbara Ann. 1990. "Bad Company: A Field Guide To Traveling with Turkeys." *Washington Post* 25 November: E3.

Daley, Christopher B. 1992. "Of Pilgrims, Meals and Myths." *Washington Post* 26 November: A39–A40.

Danbury, T. C., *et al.* 2000. "Self-selection of the analgesic drug carprofen by lame broiler chickens." *Veterinary Record* 146 (11 March): 307–311.

Davies, Brian. *Savage Luxury: The Slaughter of the Baby Seals.* 1970. London: Souvenir Press.

Davis, Karen. 1988. "The Otherness of Animals." *Between the Species: A Journal of Ethics* 4.4: 261–262. Ceased publication 1996.

_____. 1989a. "A Peaceable Kingdom for Farm Animals." *Animals' Agenda* (January): 17.

_____. 1989b. "What's Wrong with Pain Anyway?" *Animals' Agenda* (February): 50–51.

_____. 1989c. "Mixing Without Pain." *Between the Species: A Journal of Ethics* 5.1: 33–37.

_____. 1990a. "Viva, The Chicken Hen (June? – November 1985)." *Between the Species: A Journal of Ethics* 6.1: 33–35.

_____. 1990b. "Speaking for Dr. Frankenstein's Creatures Today." *Animals' Agenda* (March): 48–49.

_____. 1990c. "Savage Din, Soft Lyre and the Call of Wild Natures." *Trumpeter: Journal of Ecosophy* 7.4: 147–149. Ceased publication 1997.

_____. 1991a. "Re-Searching the Heart: An Interview with Eldon Kienholz." *Animals' Agenda* (April): 12–14.

_____. 1991b. "Cry Fowl! [Poultry Slaughter in the U.S.]." *Animals' Agenda* (April): 46–47.

_____. 1991c. "Poultry: What You Don't Know Could Kill You." *Guide To Healthy Eating* (May-June): 9–15. Washington, D.C.: Physicians Committee for Responsible Medicine.

_____. 1991d. "The Use of Poultry in Biomedical Research." *AV Magazine* (November): 6–10. Jenkintown, PA: American Anti-Vivisection Society.

_____. 1991e. "The Gore and the Gobblers." Letter. *Washington Post* 30 November: A21.

_____. 1992. "The Modern Turkey In Need of Thanksgiving Deliverance." *Animals' Agenda* (November-December): 27–28.

_____. 1992–1993. " 'We're Treated Like Animals': Women in the Poultry Industry." *Feminists for Animal Rights Newsletter* (Fall-Winter): 1, 7–8. New York: Feminists for Animal Rights.

_____. 1993a. "Personality Profile: A Chicken Named Muffie." *Humane Innovations and Alternatives* 7: 451–452. Washington Grove, MD: Psychologists for the Ethical Treatment of Animals, Inc. Ceased publication 1994.

_____. 1993b. "The Rights of Students in Courses Using Animals." *Between the Species: A Journal of Ethics* 9.3: 160–162.

_____. 1993c. "We owe poultry a painless death." *News & Observer* (Raleigh, NC) 23 November: 11A.

_____. 1994a. Testimony Before the United States House of Representatives Subcommittee on Livestock of the Committee on Agriculture Regarding the Humane Methods of Poultry Slaughter Act (HR 649), 28 September.

_____. 1994b. "Turkeys deserve a happy Thanksgiving, too." *Dallas Morning News* 20 November.

_____. 1995. "Thinking Like a Chicken: Farm Animals and the Feminine Connection." In *Animals and Women: Feminist Theoretical Explorations*, ed. Carol J. Adams and Josephine Donovan, 192–212. Durham and London: Duke UP.

_____. 1995–1996. "Expanding the Great Ape Project." *PoultryPress* (Fall-Winter): 2–3. Machipongo, VA: United Poultry Concerns, Inc.

_____. 1996a. "The Plight of Poultry." *Animals' Agenda* (July-August): 38–39.

_____. 1996b. "The Ethics of Genetic Engineering and the Futuristic Fate of Domestic Fowl." Machipongo, VA: United Poultry Concerns, Inc. www.upc-online.org.

_____. 1996c. "Thanksgiving turkeys suffer from birth to death." *Houston Chronicle* 25 November: 17A.

_____. 1996d. *Prisoned Chickens, Poisoned Eggs: An Inside Look at the Modern Poultry Industry.* Summertown, TN: Book Publishing Company.

_____. 1997. "Don't Gobble Me: The Truth Behind That Turkey on the Table." *Vegetarian Voice* (Autumn): 20–21. Dolgeville, NY: North American Vegetarian Society.

_____. 1999a. "Why Look at Birds?" *AV Magazine* (Spring): 3–5. Jenkintown, PA: American Anti-Vivisection Society.

_____. 1999b. *Instead of Chicken, Instead of Turkey: A Poultryless "Poultry" Potpourri.* Summertown, TN: Book Publishing Company.

_____. 1999c. "Chicken advocate speaks out." *Eastern Shore News* 28 August: A4.

_____. 1999d. "Diet and conditions in production make birds our prey." *Sun-Sentinel* 28 September.

_____. 1999e. "Sit down, stand up for our old fowl friend." *Philadelphia Inquirer* 25 November: A53.

_____. 2001a. "June's Story: Putting a face on the poultry trade." *Virginian-Pilot* 18 February: J3.

_____. 2001b. "Annabelle, The Baby Broiler Hen." In *Speaking Out for Animals*, ed. Kim W. Stallwood, 126–127. New York: Lantern Books.

_____. 2001c. "The Beast and the Brightest." Letter. *Village Voice* 10 April: 6.

_____. 2001d. "Chickens and Chimpanzees: the Odd Couple of the Animal Rights Movement." *Satya* (May): 16–17.

_____. 2001e. "The Difference between the Dallas Zoo and McDonald's." *Veg-News* (May-June): 10. www.vegnews.com.

Davis, S. L., and P. R. Cheeke. 1998. "Do Domestic Animals Have Minds and the Ability to Think? A Provisional Sample of Opinions on the Question." *Journal of Animal Science* 76: 2072–2079.

Dawson, Terence J., and Robert M. Herd. 1983. "Digestion In the Emu: Low Energy and Nitrogen Requirements of This Large Ratite Bird." *Comparative Biochemistry and Physiology* 75A.1: 41–45.

Dekkers, Midas. 2000. *Dearest Pet: On Bestiality.* Trans. Paul Vincent. London and New York: Verso. First published 1992.

Detienne, Marcel. 1979. *Dionysos Slain.* Trans. Mireille and Leonard Muellner. Baltimore and London: Johns Hopkins UP. First published 1977.

DeYoung, Julie. 1998. Interview with Katy Otto, 27 February.

Dickens, Charles. 1998. *A Christmas Carol and Other Haunting Tales.* New York: New York Public Library-Doubleday. First published 1843.

Dickson, James G., ed. 1992. *The Wild Turkey: Biology and Management.* Harrisburg, PA: Stackpole Books.

Donaldson, William E., *et al.* 1995. "Early poult mortality: the role of stressors and diet." *Turkey World* (January-February): 27–29.

Dorris, Michael. 1978. "Why I'm NOT Thankful for Thanksgiving." *Bulletin* 9.7: 6–9. New York: Council on Interracial Books for Children.

Drimmer, Frederick, ed. 1954. *The Animal Kingdom: The Strange and Wonderful Ways of Mammals, Birds, Reptiles, Fishes and Insects*, vol. 2. 11 vols. New York: Hawthorne Books-Greystone Press.

Dunayer, Joan. 2001. *Animal Equality: Language and Liberation.* Derwood, MD: Ryce Publishing.

Duncan, I. J. H., *et al.* 1994. "Assessment of pain associated with degenerative hip disorders in adult male turkeys." *Research in Veterinary Science* 50: 200–203.

"Early Turkey Slaughter." 1960. *Turkey Producer* (October): 19.

Eckl, Eric (eric_eckl@fws.gov). 1999. "New Partnership [with National Wild Turkey Federation] to Boost Refuge Hunting, Wildlife Watching." U.S. Fish and Wildlife Service 21 June.

Eisner, Jane R. 1998. "Will it be turkey or tofu?" *Philadelphia Inquirer* 29 November: E7.

Eisnitz, Gail A. 1997. *Slaughterhouse: The Shocking Story of Greed, Neglect, and Inhumane Treatment Inside the U.S. Meat Industry.* New York: Prometheus Books.

*Entous, Adam. 2000. Reuters. "Clinton spares 'Jerry' the turkey in annual rite, 22 November."

Evans, E. P. 1998. *The Criminal Prosecution and Capital Punishment of Animals.* Union, NJ: The Lawbook Exchange, Ltd. First published 1906.

Farb, JoAnn. 2000. *Compassionate Souls: Raising the Next Generation to Change the World.* New York: Lantern Books.

Fehr, Stephen C. 1991. "A Family Trip to the Farm Ends in Murder Most Fowl." *Washington Post* 24 November: B1, B3.

Feinberg, Andrew. 1984. "Carve Only in a Fowl Mood." *New York Times* 22 November: A27.

Feltwell, Ray. 1953. *Turkey Farming.* London: Faber and Faber.

Fletcher, Sherrie M. Archivist, Ronald Reagan Presidential Library. 1998. Letter to David J. Cantor, 30 October.

*Fountain, John W. 1995. "Chickens Come First in Her Pecking Order." *Washington Post* 31 August: C3.

Fox, Michael Allen. 1993. "Environmental Ethics and the Ideology of Meat Eating." *Between the Species: A Journal of Ethics* 9.3: 121–132.

_____. 1999. *Deep Vegetarianism.* Philadelphia: Temple UP.

Fox, Nicols. 1998. *Spoiled: Why Our Food Is Making Us Sick and What We Can Do About It.* New York: Penguin. First published 1997.

Fritz, Mark. 1995. Associated Press. "Turkey industry in trouble: Top-heavy superbirds are causing problems." *USA Today* 21 November: 7A.

Frost, Robert. 1969. Home Burial. *The Poetry of Robert Frost*, ed. Edward Connery Lathem, 51–55. New York: Holt, Rinehart and Winston. Poem first published 1914.

Garreau, Joel. 1992. "The Day of the Family: Thanksgiving Rituals Served with Relish." *Washington Post* 26 November: A1, A41.

Gibson, Charles. 1964. *The Aztecs Under Spanish Rule: A History of the Indians of the Valley of Mexico 1519–1810*. Stanford: Stanford UP.

Girard, René. 1987. "Generative Scapegoating; Girard Paper: Discussion." In *Violent Origins: Ritual Killing and Cultural Formation*, ed. Robert G. Hammerton-Kelly, 73–145. Stanford: Stanford UP.

*Glass. Ira. 1996; 1997; *1998; 1999. "Poultry Slam." *This American Life*. PRI. WBEZ Chicago. November 29; December 5; *November 28; November 26.

Glickman, Dan. 1999. Release No. 0292.99: Remarks as Prepared for Delivery by Secretary of Agriculture Dan Glickman [at] National Turkey Federation Summer Meeting, Washington, D.C. 20 July. USDA Web site.

Goldoftas, Barbara. 1989. "Inside the Slaughterhouse." *Southern Exposure: A Journal of Politics & Culture* 17.2: 25–29.

Goodman, Ellen. 1992. "The Seasonal Equivalent of Quality Time." *Sun* (Baltimore) 26 November: 31A.

Green, Jonathon. 1996. *Slang Through the Ages*. Lincolnshire, IL: NTC Publishing Group.

Greenstone, Julius H. 1946. *Jewish Feasts and Fasts*. New York: Bloch Publishing Co.

Grein, Tom. 1997. "Holidays and Turkey Bashing." *Observer* (Herndon, VA) 21 November: 10.

Grzimek, Bernhard, ed. 1972. *Grzimek's Animal Life Encyclopedia*. Vol. 8. New York: Van Nostrand Reinhold. First published 1968.

"Guess Who's NOT Coming to Dinner." 1985. *New York Times* 24 November: A66.

Hagenbaugh, Barbara. 1998. Reuters. "Vegetarians gobbling tofu turkey products this Thanksgiving." *Seattle Times/Post Intelligencer* 15 November.

Hale, E. B., *et al.* 1975. "The Behaviour of Turkeys." In *Behaviour of Domestic Animals*, ed. E.S.E. Hafez, 554–592. 3rd ed. Baltimore: Williams and Wilkins Co.

Hall, Evelyn. 1995. "Larison's stirs Thanksgiving thoughts." *Weekend Plus; now North Jersey Newspaper* (Somerville, NJ) 15–17 November: 4–5.

_____. 1998. Phone interview with author, 8 June.

Hall, Rebecca. 1984. *Voiceless Victims*. Middlesex: Wildwood House Ltd.

Hanks III, Douglas. 1999. "Move Over Turkey." *Washington Post* 21 November: M1.

Hannum, Alberta Pierson. 1938. "Turkey Hunt." In *The Best Short Stories 1938 and the Yearbook of the American Short Story*, ed. Edward J. O'Brien, 146–152. Boston and New York: Riverside Press-Houghton Mifflin.

Hardy, Thomas. 1912. *Tess of the d'Urbervilles*. Ch. 15. Vol. I of *The Works of Thomas Hardy in Prose and Verse*. 1984. New York: AMS Press. First published 1891.

_____. 1975. *Jude The Obscure*. Part 1, Ch. 10. Intro. Terry Eagleton. London: MacMillan. First published 1896.

Harris, Marvin. 1977. *Cannibals and Kings: The Origins of Cultures*. New York: Random House.

Hartley, Dorothy, and Margaret M. Elliot. 1926. *Life and Work of the People of England: A Pictorial Record from Contemporary Sources.* Vol. 2 (The Renaissance A.D. 1500–1800) of "People's Life & Work" Series. London: B.T. Batsford.

Haun. Mildred. 1968. "The Turkey Feather." In *The Hawk's Done and Other Stories*, ed. Herschel Gower. TN: Vanderbilt UP.

Hayes, Paul G. 1995. "Who's the turkey?" *Milwaukee Journal Sentinel* 30 April: 13.

Healy, William M. 1992. "Behavior." In *The Wild Turkey: Biology and Management*, ed. James G. Dickson, 46–65. Harrisburg, PA: Stackpole Books.

Heath, G. B. S. 1984. "The Slaughter of Broiler Chickens." *World Poultry Science Association Journal* 40.2: 151.

Heberlein, James A. 1997. Letter to author, 13 October.

Hening. Robin Marantz. 1998. "Creating holiday traditions is no walk in the park." *USA Today* 25 November: 27A.

Henry, James S. 1990. "Why I Hate Christmas." *New Republic* 31 December: 21–24.

*Highet, Alistair. 1994. "Activists Are on the Outs With Turkey Races at Inn." *Litchfield County Times* 18 November: 1, 7.

*_____. 1997. "'Turkey Olympics' is Canceled By Inn; Based on Protests." *Litchfield County Times* 21 November: 1, 7.

Hindi, Steve. 1995a. "CHARK Attack: Turkey Shoot Exposed by Undercover Video Sting!" *News Letter* 5 July. Chicago Animal Rights Coalition.

_____. 1995b. "Victory In Transylvania!" *News Letter*, 23 October. Chicago Animal Rights Coalition.

"History of the Turkey." 1960. *Turkey Producer* (October): 8, 20.

Hoban, Lillian. 1990. *Silly Tilly's Thanksgiving Dinner.* Columbus, OH: Newfield Publications-HarperCollins.

Hobsbawn, Eric, and Terence Ranger, eds. 1983. *The Invention of Tradition.* Cambridge: Cambridge UP.

Holtzhausen, Anita, and Marlene Kitze. 1990. *The Ostrich.* Oudtshoorn, Republic of South Africa: C. P. Nel Museum.

Howitt, William. 1844. *The Rural Life of England.* 3rd ed. London: Longman, Brown, Green, and Longmans.

Hulsizer v. Labor Day Committee, Inc. 1999. J-76–1999. Pennsylvania Supreme Court 21 July.

"Humane Methods of Slaughter Act." Title 7 U.S. Code Sections 1901–1906. Detailed Regulations and Enforcement. Title 9 CFR (Code of Federal Regulations). Part 313. Sections 313.1–313.90.

Hutto, Joe. 1995. *Illumination in the Flatwoods: A Season with the Wild Turkey.* New York: Lyons & Burford.

Ickis, Marguerite. 1964. *The Book of Festive Holidays.* New York: Dodd, Mead & Co.

Irwin, R. Stephen. 1984. *Hunters of the Eastern Forest.* The Native Hunter Series. BC and WA: Hancock House.

Jamieson, Dale. 1985. "Against Zoos." In *In Defense of Animals*, ed. Peter Singer, 108–117. New York: Basil Blackwell.

Johnson, Andrew. 1991. *Factory Farming*. Cambridge: Basil Blackwell.

Jolley, H. Scott. 2001. "Chicken Run." *Travel and Leisure* (February): 45–46, 48.

Jones, P .E. 1965. *The Worshipful Company of Poulters of the City of London: A Short History*. London: Oxford UP. First published 1939.

Jones, Tamara. 1996. "The Stuffing of Scandal In Which We Find Juicy Tidbits About the National Turkey." *Washington Post* 28 November: B1–B2, B17.

*_____. 1999. "For the Birds." *Washington Post* 14 November: F1, F4–F5.

Jordan, Tracy. 1995a. "Turkey shoots under fire." *Morning Call* (Allentown, PA) 28 September B1, B8.

_____. 1995b. "Hunting club cancels live turkey shoot." *Morning Call* 10 October: B3.

Josselyn, John, Colonial Traveler. 1988. A Critical Edition of *Two Voyages to New-England*, ed. Paul J. Lindholdt. Hanover, NH: University Press of New England. First published 1674.

Jukes, Thomas H. 1992. Letter to author, 4 September.

Jull, Morley A. 1930. "Fowls of Forest and Stream Tamed by Man." *National Geographic Magazine* (March): 326–371.

Kane, David. 1990. News Release, 18 November.

Karr, Kathleen. 1997. "Turkey Talk." *Washington Post* 27 November: D5.

_____. 1998. *The Great Turkey Walk*. New York: Farrar, Straus and Giroux.

Kaye, Natalie. 1999. "Vary the Vegetables: Five Ways To Compete With the Meat." *Washington Post* 21 November: M1.

Kelly, Matt. 1994. "Gilda and Ted." *PoultryPress* (Fall-Winter): 4. Machipongo, VA: United Poultry Concerns, Inc.

Kisserly, Kelly P. 1991. Associated Press. "We're still trying to picture turkeys moving on treadmills." *Times Tribune* 20 November. Nation.

Kleeman, Terry, and Marie Gleason. 2001. Boris. Poem. *PoultryPress* (Summer): 2. Machipongo, VA: United Poultry Concerns, Inc.

Knowlson, T. Sharper. 1968. *The Origins of Popular Superstitions and Customs*. London: T. Werner Laurie Ltd. First published 1910.

Kuykendall, James R., and Elizabeth S. Howard. 1985. "Turkey Trot Days at Oliver Hall's Store." *Alabama Review* 38.2: 105–118.

*Lavoie, Denise. 1997. "Turkey games called off after event ruffles feathers." Associated Press. *Greenwich Time* (CT) 26 November.

Leach, Edmund. 1964. "Anthropological Aspects of Language: Animal Categories and Verbal Abuse." In *New Directions in the Study of Language*, ed. Eric H. Lennenberg, 32–63. Cambridge: MIT Press.

Lears, Jackson. 1997. "Inventing a Tradition for Every Occasion." *Washington Post* 7 December: C3.

Le Guin, Ursula. 1985. "She Unnames Them." *New Yorker* 21 January: 27.

"The Light and Dark Sides of Thanksgiving Turkey." 1973. *Moneysworth: The Consumer Newsletter* 4.4 (26 November): 1–2.

Linzey, Andrew. 1998. "Honoring the Flesh." *Animals' Agenda* (November-December): 21.

_____. 1999. *Animal Rites: Liturgies of Animal Care.* London: SCM Press.

Loewen, James W. 1995. *Lies My Teacher Told Me: Everything Your American History Textbook Got Wrong.* New York: Touchstone-Simon & Schuster.

Lorenz, Konrad Z. 1952. *King Solomon's Ring: New Light on Animal Ways.* Forward Julian Huxley. New York: Thomas Y. Crowell.

Love, W. DeLoss. 1895. *The Fast and Thanksgiving Days of New England.* Boston and New York: Houghton, Mifflin and Co.

Luke, Brian A. 1998. "Media and Turkeys." Email to Chickadee-1@envirolink.org, 28 November.

Lum, Khalid. 1992. "Talking Turkey." *Hartford Advocate* (CT) 26 November: 14.

Mac Donald, Heather. 2000. *The Burden of Bad Ideas: How Modern Intellectuals Misshape Our Society.* Chicago: Ivan R. Dee.

Mackay, Charles. 1859. *Life and Liberty in America: or, Sketches of a Tour in the United States and Canada in 1857–8.* New York: Harper & Brothers.

Mackey, Mary. Turkeys. 1999. In Carolyn J. Christman and Robert O. Hawes. *Birds of a Feather: Saving Rare Turkeys From Extinction.* Pittsboro, NC: American Livestock Breeds Conservancy.

Madson, John. 1990. "Once, he was almost a 'goner' but now Old Tom's a 'comer.'" *Smithsonian* (May): 54–62.

Malcolmson, Robert W. 1973. *Popular Recreations in English Society 1700–1850.* Cambridge: Cambridge UP.

Manning, Anita. 2000. "FDA, turkey farmers debate health of feast." *USA Today* 20 November: 10D.

Marchetti, John. 1996. "Ballet Leads Student to Science Lab." *Harvard College Gazette* (Fall): 9.

Markham, Gervase. 1986. *The English Housewife: Containing the inward and outward virtues which ought to be in a complete woman...,*ed. Michael R. Best. Montreal & Kingston: McGill-Queen's UP. First published 1615.

Marsden, Stanley J., and J. Holmes Martin. 1939. *Turkey Management.* Danville, IL: The Interstate.

*Marshall, Bradley. 1997. "Living at Thanksgiving." *Washington Times* 27 November: A1; Washington Weekend, M4–M6.

Mason, Jim, and Peter Singer. 1990. *Animal Factories.* New York: Harmony Books. First published 1980.

_____. 1993. *An Unnatural Order: Uncovering the Roots of Our Domination of Nature and Each Other.* New York: Simon & Schuster.

_____("Frank Observer"). 1994. "In the Turkey Breeding Factory." *PoultryPress* (Fall-Winter): 1–2, 7. Machipongo, VA: United Poultry Concerns, Inc.

Masson, Jeffrey Moussaieff, and Susan McCarthy. 1995. *When Elephants Weep: The Emotional Lives of Animals*. New York: Delacorte Press.

Mercia, Leonard S. 1981. *Raising Your Own Turkeys*. Pownal, VT: Garden Way Publishing-Storey Communications.

Merrit, John B. 1996. "The Turkey Industry." In *American Poultry History 1974–1993*, ed. John L. Skinner, 128–136. Vol. II. Mount Morris, IL: Watt Publishing Co.

Mesick, Jane Louise. 1922. *The English Traveller in America 1785–1835*. Westport, CT: Greenwood Press.

Messina, Debbie. 1998. "I–264 will no longer be a turkey." *Virginian-Pilot* 25 November: A1, A12.

Miller, Deborah. 1992. "Next Year in Tofu-Land. Poem." *Jewish Vegetarians* (Winter). Federalsburg, MD: Jewish Vegetarians of North America.

Miller, Henry. 1962. Henry David Thoreau, 111–118. In *Stand Still Like the Hummingbird*, 111–118. New York: New Directions.

Mitchell, J. David. 1958. "What Is a Turkey and Where Did It Come From?" *Turkey Producer* (September): 20–21.

Mizejewski, Gerald. 1998. "Breeder talks turkey." *Washington Times* 25 November: C6.

Montgomery, David. 2000. "Not Quite a Slice of Poultry Paradise: Pardoned Turkeys Live a Lonely Life." *Washington Post* 24 November: B1, B7.

Moore, James. 1999. "Avian Intelligence: Who You Callin' Bird Brain?" *Healthy Pet* (Fall): 30.

Motolinia, Torilio de. 1951. *Motolinia's History of the Indians of New Spain*. Trans. Francis Borgia Steck. Washington, D.C.: Academy of American Franciscan History.

Munro, Alice. 1983. "The Turkey Season." In *The Moons of Jupiter*, 60–76. New York: Alfred A. Knopf.

Naughton, Jim. 1988. "The Turkey Ritual: Stuff It!" *Washington Post* 19 November: C8.

Nestor, Felicia, and Wenonah Hauter. 2000. *The Jungle 2000: Is America's Meat Fit To Eat?* Washington, D.C.: Public Citizen. www.citizen.org/cmep.

Nichol, John Thomas, ed. 1990. "Holidays and Holy Days." *Encyclopedia Americana*. Vol. 14.

Nicol, Christine, and Marian Stamp Dawkins. 1990. "Homes fit for hens." *New Scientist* (17 March): 46–51.

O'Connor, Flannery. 1971. "The Turkey." In *The Complete Stories*, 42–53. New York: Farrar, Straus and Giroux.

O'Hara, Chris. 1994. Letter to author, 14 November.

Orwell, George. 1945. "Politics and the English Language." In *Shooting an Elephant and Other Essays*, 77–92. New York: Harcourt, Brace and Co.

Otto, Katy. 1998. "The Truth Behind the Pardoning Ceremony." English 429 Independent Study (3 May): 1–8. College Park: University of Maryland.

Ovid. 1961. *Metamorphoses*. Trans. Rolfe Humphries. Bloomington: Indiana UP.

Partridge, Eric. 1984. *A Dictionary of Slang and Unconventional English*, ed. Paul Beale. London: Routledge & Kegan Paul.

Pattison, Mark, ed. 1993. *The Health of Poultry*. Ames: Iowa State UP.

Patty. 1998. "Turkey Sacrifice." Email to Chickadee-1@envirolink.org, 30 November.

Pearce, Michael. 1995. "Wild Turkeys Strut and Multiply." *Wall Street Journal* 16 August: A8.

_____. 1999. "Gobbling Up the Grand Slam." *Wall Street Journal* 12 May: A20.

Pearson, Charles D. 1947. "To Carve a Turkey." *New York Times* 23 November: 42.

*Perl, Peter. 1995. "The Truth About Turkeys." *Washington Post Magazine* 24 November: 14–16, 36–39.

_____. 2000. "Outbreak." *Washington Post Magazine* 16 January: 8–13, 20–27.

Perry, Charles. 1996. "It's Curtains, Turkey." *Los Angeles Times* 24 November: H10.

PETA (People for the Ethical Treatment of Animals). 1999. "Pig Cruelty Exposed." www.goveg.com/pig case.html.

_____. 1999. "Turkey-Farm Cruelty Expose." www.peta.org/feat/nc/index.html.

Peterson, William J. 1968. "Thanksgiving in America." *Palimpsest* 49.12: 545–555.

*Philip, Rowan. 2000. "Of Poultry and Presidents: One Resilient Male Pardons Another." *Washington Post* 23 November: C1, C16.

Pilkey, Dav. 1990. *'Twas the Night Before Thanksgiving*. New York: Orchard Books.

Pleck, Elizabeth H. 2000. *Celebrating the Family: Ethnicity, Consumer Culture, and Family Rituals*. Cambridge: Harvard UP.

Porphyry (3rd Century, A.D.). 1965. *On Abstinence From Animal Food*. Trans. Thomas Taylor. Ed., Intro. Esme Wynne-Tyson. London & Fontwell: Centaur Press Ltd.

*Post, Todd. 1996. "When Animal Rights Collide With Thanksgiving Appetites." *Takoma Voice* (MD) November: 12–13, 15, 27.

"President Gets Prize Turkey." 1948. *New York Times* 24 November: 17.

"President Gets a Turkey and Plea to Use Mercy." 1956. *New York Times* 20 November: 31.

*Pressley, Sue Anne. 1991. "At This Thanksgiving Table, They Serve Turkey Diners: Vegetarian Couple's Pet Fowl Get to Do the Gobbling." *Washington Post* 27 November: D1.

Proctor, Stuart. 1998. Interview with Katy Otto, 15 April.

Prosise, Everette M. 1999. Letter. *Virginia Tech Magazine* (Fall): 2.

*Pryor, Diane. 1995. "A Vegetarian Feast." *Morning Herald* (Hagerstown, MD) 15 November: C1.

Purdom, Janie (President, Yellville Area Chamber of Commerce). 1996. Letter to author, 29 October.

*Rathner, Janet. 1996. "Where chickens come home to roost." *Potomac Gazette* (MD) 4 September: A1, A11.

*_____. 1997. "United Poultry Concerns wants to nest elsewhere." *Potomac Gazette* (MD) 13 August: A4–A5.

Rather, Dan. 1996. "So What if It's a Turkey? It's Ours. It's Family." *New York Times* 25 December: A26.

Rawson, Hugh. 1989. *Wicked Words: A Treasury of Curses, Insults, Put-Downs, and Other Formerly Unprintable Terms from Anglo-Saxon Times to the Present.* New York: Crown Publishers.

Reagan, Ronald. 1981. "Remarks to Reporters Upon Receiving a Thanksgiving Turkey from the National Turkey Federation." *Administration of Ronald Reagan*, 18 November. 1069–1070. Washington, D.C.: The White House.

_____. 1987. "Informal Exchange With Reporters: Thanksgiving Turkey. 1987." *Administration of Ronald Reagan*, 23 November: 1376–1377. Washington, D.C.: The White House.

Reel, Monte. 2000. "Turkeys Reclaiming Md. Woods: Elusive Wild Birds Get Humans' Help." *Washington Post* 23 November: B1, B7.

"Reluctant Guest at White House." 1984. *New York Times* 17 November: A1.

Riordan, Teresa. 1997. "Patents: New techniques for raising and killing turkeys arrive just in time for Thanksgiving." *New York Times* 24 November: D2.

Roberts, Roxanne. 1991. "Trotting Out the Turkey." *Washington Post* 26 November: B1, B8.

Rockwell, Norman. 1943. "Thanksgiving (*Freedom from Want*)." *Saturday Evening Post* (27 November). Cover.

Rodman, Frances. 1954. "Fuss 'n' Feathers: Literary tidbits on the pleasures—and perils—of Thanksgiving feasts." *New York Times Magazine* 21 November: 17.

Roeper, Richard. 2000. "Silverstone's bold stand for the rights of turkeys." *Chicago Sun-Times* 22 November: 11.

Rogers, Lesley J. 1995. *The Development of Brain and Behaviour in the Chicken.* Wallingford (UK): Cab International.

_____. 1997. *Minds Of Their Own: Thinking and Awareness in Animals.* Boulder: Westview Press.

Rogers, Lesley J., and Gisela Kaplan. 2000. *Songs, Roars, and Rituals: Communication in Birds, Mammals, and Other Animals.* Cambridge: Harvard UP.

Root, Waverly, and Richard de Rochemont. 1976. *Eating In America: A History.* New York: William Morrow & Co.

"Romania: What Happened To The Children." 1997. *Turning Point*, 16 January. NY: ABC News. Transcript #174.

Rountree, Helen C. 1989. *The Powhatan Indians of Virginia: Their Traditional Culture.* Norman: University of Oklahoma Press.

Rule, Ann, 1983. *Possession.* New York: Pocket Books-Simon & Schuster.

Ryder, Richard D. 1989. *Animal Revolution: Changing Attitudes towards Speciesism.* Cambridge: Basil Blackwell.

Safire, William. 1980. *On Language.* New York: Times Books.

Sagan, Eli. 1974. *Cannibalism: Human Aggression and Cultural Form.* New York: The Psychohistory Press.

Sanders, William T., *et al.* 1979. *The Basin of Mexico: Ecological Processes in the Evolution of a Civilization*. New York: Academic Press-Harcourt Brace Jovanovich.

Schlein, Miriam. 1989. *Pigeons*. New York: Thomas Y. Crowell.

Schlesinger, Allison. 2000. "Turkeys can be fowl critters." Associated Press. *Tribune Review* (Pittsburgh) 22 November: A4.

Schlosser, Eric. 2001a. "Why McDonald's Fries Taste So Good." *Atlantic Monthly* (January): 50–56.

_____. 2001b. *Fast Food Nation*. New York: Houghton Mifflin.

Schorger, A. W. 1961. "An Ancient Pueblo Turkey." *The Auk: A Quarterly Journal of Ornithology*. 78.2: 138–144.

_____. 1966. *The Wild Turkey: Its History and Domestication*. Norman: University of Oklahoma Press.

Schramm, W.P. 1962. "The ByGone Turkey Drover." *Turkey Producer* (August): 21.

Schroeder, Albert H. 1968. "Birds and Feathers in Documents Relating To Indians of the Southwest." *Papers of the Archaeological Society of New Mexico* I: 95–114.

Shell, Ellen Ruppel. 2001. "New World Syndrome: Spam and turkey tails turned Micronesians into Macronesians: A Case Study of how fatty Western plenty is taking a disastrous toll on people in developing countries." *Atlantic Monthly* (June): 50–53.

Sherrill, Martha. 1989. "The Gift of Gobble: Bush & the National Thanksgiving Bird." *Washington Post* 18 November: C1, C2.

*Shockley, Ted. 1998. "'Mother Hen' moves her brood and chicken advocacy group to Machipongo." *Eastern Shore News* (VA) 26 September: A1, A7.

*"Show some respect for turkeys." 1995. Editorial. *Hartford Courant* 6 May: A12.

Sickel, H.S. 1940. *History of Thanksgiving and Proclamations*. Philadelphia: International Printing Co.

Singer, Peter. 1990. *Animal Liberation*. New York: New York Review Book Random House. First published 1975.

_____. 1994. *Rethinking Life and Death: The Collapse of Our Traditional Ethics*. New York: St. Martin's Press.

_____. 1999. *A Darwinian Left: Potitics, Evolution and Cooperation*. New Haven and London: Yale UP.

"Singled Out: Tom and Michele." 1982. Editorial. *New York Times* 30 November: 30.

Skewes, Peter, and Glenn Birrenkott. 1993. "Turkey stunning: limit amperage to minimize cardiac fibrillation." *Turkey World* (April-May): 24–26.

Skinner, John L., *et al.*, eds. 1974. *American Poultry History 1823–1973*. Vol. I. Madison, WI: American Printing & Publishing—American Poultry Historical Society, Inc.

Skutch, Alexander F. 1996. *The Minds of Birds*. College Station: Texas A&M UP.

Small, M.C. 1974. "Turkeys." In *American Poultry History 1823–1973*, ed. John L. Skinner, *et al.*, 434–469. Vol. I. Madison, WI: American Printing and Publishing—American Poultry Historical Society, Inc.

Smith, Gene (H. E.). 1986. "The Editor's Notebook: The Rest of the Ben Franklin Story." *Turkey Call* (November-December): 4.

Smith, Helen Evertson. 1966. *Colonial Days and Ways: As Gathered from Family Papers.* New York: Frederick Ungar Publishing Co. First published 1900.

Smith, Page, and Charles Daniel. 2000. *The Chicken Book.* Athens: University of Georgia Press. First published 1975.

Solomon, Mary Jane. 1997. "At Thanksgiving, Poultry in Motion." *Washington Post Weekend* 21 November: 67.

Soustelle, Jacques. 1962. *The Daily Life of the Aztecs On the Eve of the Spanish Conquest.* New York: Macmillan.

Sowell, Randy. Archivist, Harry S. Truman Library. 1998. Letter to the author, 13 August.

Stahlberg, Mike. 1996. "Turkey shoots steeped in tradition." *The Register-Guard* (Eugene, OR): 1D, 5D.

"State of Minnesota, County of Chaska v. Mark Christian Lund." 2001. T8–01–2992. Judicial Court, First District 31 May.

Sterba, James P. 2001. "This Thanksgiving, It Could Be the Turkeys Doing the Celebrating." *Wall Street Journal* 31 May: A1, A6.

Stout, David. 1996. "They Sit and Wait So Others Can Serve." *New York Times* 24 November: E3.

*Studebaker, Michele. 1992. "Activists target local farm in turkey-killing protest." *Loudoun Times-Mirror* (Leesburg, VA) 25 November: A1, A17.

Sugarman, Carole. 1994a. "Agency Report Faults 40 Percent of Largest U.S. Turkey Processors." *Washington Post* 5 February: A3.

_____. 1994b. "Fowl Play." *Washington Post* 3 August: E1, E11.

Tanzer, Deborah. 1998. "Tanzer on Turkeys." Email to Djcgside@aol.org, 30 November.

Taylor, Ella. 2001. "Film: The 2000 Ella Awards." *Atlantic Monthly* (April): 34.

Taylor, Holly. 2000. Conversation with author. October 5.

Teale, Edwin Way, ed. 1954. *The Wilderness World of John Muir.* Boston: Houghton Mifflin.

Terkel, Studs. 1986. *Hard Times: An Oral History of the Great Depression.* New York: The New Press. First published 1970.

"Thanksgiving: What Did the Pilgrims Have that We Haven't Got? The Key to Happiness—And Survival." 1947. Editorial. *Life* 24 November: 38.

Thomas, Keith. 1983. *Man and the Natural World: A History of the Modern Sensibility.* New York: Pantheon Books.

*Thornton, Robert. 1991. "Animal activist lobbies to stop fowl play." *Montgomery Journal* (MD): 30 August: A4.

"Tip-Up Town rolls out the turkeys [bowling with frozen turkeys]." 2001. *Bay City Times* (MI) 29 January.

Trillin, Calvin. 1982. "The Case of the Purloined Turkey." In *Uncivil Liberties*, 111–114. New Haven and New York: Ticknor & Fields.

Trollope, Frances, Milton. 1949. *Domestic Manners of the Americans*, ed. Donald Smalley. New York: Alfred A. Knopf. First published 1832.

Trueheart, Charles. 1992. "Gobbler Getaway: The National Turkey, From Fleeting Fame To Muddy Pasture." *Washington Post* 26 November: B1, B6.

"Turkey." 1989 ed. *Oxford English Dictionary*. Vol. 18.

"Turkey Shoot Shot Down by Undercover Video Sting." 1995–1996. *PoultryPress* (Fall-Winter): 7. Machipongo, VA: United Poultry Concerns.

"Turkey Trivia, Tidbits and Teasers." N.d. Web Page. National Turkey Federation, Courtesy of the U.S. Department of Agriculture.

"Turkeys." 1993. In *Hidden Suffering*, ed. Clare Druce, 23–30. Holmfirth, Huddersfield, U.K.: Farm Animal Welfare Network.

*"Turkeys." 1998. Commentary. *Virginian-Pilot* 22 November: J1, J3, J6.

"Turkeys For the President's Christmas Dinner. 1998." *New York Times* 14 December: 34.

UPI (United Press International). 1970. "Turkey's Eyes Soften the President's Heart." *New York Times* 25 November: 22.

USDA/NASS (U.S. Department of Agriculture/National Agricultural Statistics Service). 2001. "Livestock Slaughter 2000 Summary (March); Poultry Slaughter 2000 Summary (April)." www.usda.gov/nass. Publications.

Vaillant, y George C. 1941. *Aztecs of Mexico: Origin, Rise and Fall of the Aztec Nation* New York: Doubleday, Doran & Co.

Visser, Margaret. 1992a. *The Rituals of Dinner: The Origins, Evolution, Eccentricities, and Meaning of Table Manners*. New York: Penguin. First published 1991.

_____. One Strange Bird. 1992b. *New York Times* 26 November: A27.

Walsh, Sharon. 1998. "Hosts Around Nation Thankful—for Takeout." *Washington Post* 26 November: A3.

Watson, George C. 1901. *Farm Poultry: A Popular Sketch of Domestic Fowls for the Farmer and Amateur*, 3rd ed. Rural Science Series. New York: Macmillan.

Webster's Third New International Dictionary of the English Language Unabridged. 1993.

Weiss, Rick. 1997. "Techno Turkeys." *Washington Post* 12 November: H1, H7

Wentworth, Harold, and Stuart Berg Flexner. 1960. *Dictionary of American Slang*. New York: Thomas Y. Crowell.

White, Bailey. 1993. "Turkeys." In *Mama Makes Up Her Mind: And Other Dangers of Southern Living, 12–16*. Reading, MA: Addison-Wesley Publishing Company.

White, Ben. 2000. "Hotline Hums Well After the Thanksgiving Turkey's Done." *Washington Post* 23 November: A41.

White, E.B. 1944. "Security." In *One Man's Meat*, 13–17. New York: Harper & Row.

Wickersham, Marion. 1990. "A Tale of Two Turkeys." *Sanctuary News* (Fall): 2. Watkins Glen, NY: Farm Sanctuary.

Wilbur, Richard. 1956. "A Black November Turkey." Poem. In *Things of This World*, 10–11. New York: Harcourt, Brace & World.

Williams, Joy. 1997. "The Inhumanity of the Animal People." *Harper's Magazine* (August): 60–67.

Williams, Marjorie. 1987. "Watch the Birdie! At the White House, It's Pressed Turkey." *Washington Post* 24 November: D1, D9.

Willison, George F. 1945. *Saints and Strangers: Being the Lives of the Pilgrim Fathers & Their Families...*New York: Reynal & Hitchcock.

Winchell, Walter. 1927. *Vanity Fair* (November): 67, 132, 134.

Wise, Steven M. 2000. *Rattling The Cage: Toward Legal Rights for Animals*. Cambridge: Perseus Books.

"World Meat Production Rising Faster Than Human Population." 1961. Editorial. *Turkey Producer* (January): 4.

Wright, Albert Hazen. 1914. "Early Records of the Wild Turkey." *The Auk: A Quarterly Journal of Ornithology* 31.3: 334–358.

Yardley, Jonathan. 1995. "Gobble Squabble." *Washington Post* 20 November: D2.

Yorke, Jeffrey. 1990. "Bush and the Bird at Hand." *Washington Post Magazine*. 11 November: 13.

*Zabarenko, Deborah. 1996. "Thanksgiving a nightmare for friends of the turkey." Reuters. 27 November.

Zucco, Tom. 1999. "A turkey of a tradition." *St. Petersburg Times* 17 November: 3D, 6D.

Index ⌇